THE *Mobile* Groomer's BIBLE

Mary Oquendo &

Beth Cristiano

spirited dog
PRODUCTIONS

WorkingChihuahua Press

WorkingChihuahua Press
Sequim, WA
www.SpiritedDog.com

LCCN 2019903683
Print ISBN 978-0-9828831-4-3
Ebook ISBN 978-0-9828831-5-0

Front Cover Design: Alchemic Creations
Back Cover Design: M. G. Saloff
Other images include Chalabala and fotoedu/iStockPhotos.com
Interior Design: J. L. Saloff

v. 1.00
First Edition, 2019
Printed on acid free paper in the USA.

Contents

Forward 1
From Mary 5
From Beth 6

START YOUR BUSINESS 7
Are You Sure You Want to Do This? 9
Research 10
Putting It on Paper 13
SWOT Analysis 15
Vehicle Choices 20
Franchising 22

SUPPORT YOUR BUSINESS 27
Support Systems 29
Professional Support 30
Continuing Your Education 33
Supporting Materials 36
Retirement 40

CONTROL YOUR BUSINESS 41
Setting Client Expectations and Boundaries 43
Pricing and Number of Pets Needed 48
Routing and Scheduling 52
Forms 55
Mobile Groomer Vehicle Safety 57
Pet Safety 63
Personal Wellbeing and Safety 66
Sanitation 68
Spares 74
Security 76

Payment Options 79
Going on the Go 81
Pet First Aid Kits 82

LOVE YOUR BUSINESS. **87**
Niche Yourself. 89
Love Your Vehicle. 92
Love Yourself 94
Love Your Business 97
Storing and Winterizing Your Vehicle 99

LISTEN TO YOUR BUSINESS **101**
What Do Your Clients Want? 103
Educated Clients Are Good Clients 107
Showcase Yourself 110
Marketing 112
Press Release 122
Live Events 124
Retail 128

IMAGINE WHERE YOUR BUSINESS CAN TAKE YOU . **131**
Document Your Process 133
Organizational Chart. 136
Employees Yes Or No? 138
Help Wanted! 140
Applicants and the Hiring Process 143
Legal Requirements 149
New Hire Orientation 150
Handbooks. 154
Training Employees 157
Worker Classification 161
Employee Compensation 163
Discipline and Termination. 166

COME FULL CIRCLE **171**
    What's Your Endgame? 173
    Selling Your Mobile Unit 178

PARTING THOUGHTS **183**
    Mary's Parting Thoughts 185
    Beth's Parting Thoughts 187

RESOURCES **189**
    Resources and Forms 191

Forward

Over the course of my 35 years in the pet grooming industry, I have worked in private salons, at a huge boarding kennel, at an upscale spa, and for veterinarians. I was an early pioneer in house call grooming, and for a happy time I was a Mobile Pet Stylist. As a mobile groomer, I did almost everything wrong, but still enjoyed it tremendously. I had profitable business and happy customers. However, I would have made far less mistakes, had fewer frustrations, and even happier customers if I'd had a book like this to help guide me.

I first met Mary and Beth many years ago at a grooming convention. I was there giving grooming demonstrations and as a lecturer, and they were there teaching pet first aid. I heard many favorable comments about their classes, so made a point to go say hello and introduce myself. From that meeting lovely, lasting friendships were formed.

It is was my great honor to read pages of this book as they were writing it. I was impressed to find that they managed to cover everything from planning and starting a mobile business to looking ahead towards preparing for retirement. There is even a helpful chapter on employees, something I have not seen in other mobile guides.

You will be certain to learn much when you read chapters filled with knowledge gleaned from the combined wisdom of 45-plus years immersed in the mobile pet grooming industry. Mary and Beth consolidated their hard-won wisdom into crisp, easy-to-read sections. There is a strong focus on the business side of grooming, an area often overlooked in our industry.

If you are considering a career as a mobile pet stylist, or already are one but want to sharpen your game, this book will be of help. If you want your mobile business to include miles of smiles, add this book to your "must read" list.

Daryl Conner, Master Pet Stylist, Meritus, Master Cat Groomer, author of *101 Tips for Real World Groomers* and co-author with Mary Oquendo of *Holistic Pet Grooming*. Recipient of multiple Cardinal Crystal awards and the Barkleigh Honors award for journalism. Owner, FairWinds Grooming Studio, Appleton, ME.

I sure could've used a book like this when I first started mobile grooming in 2007! It's comprehensive and detailed, yet written in a way that anyone can understand. Mary and Beth bring years of business experience and grooming wisdom together to create a definitive guide to becoming a successful mobile groomer.

They approach the business from all aspects, and provide clear guidance on nurturing and growing your mobile grooming business, regardless of what your goals may be. Whether you're a franchisee or a solo operation, this book has all the information you'll need, from marketing and advertising to maintenance and taxes.

I highly recommend this book to anyone who is exploring the idea of becoming a professional mobile groomer.

~ Lori Monian, Lori's Grooming, Paradise, CA

From Mary

I got my start in grooming in 1999 when I went to work as a bather for a nationally-branded company. I will forever be grateful to them for introducing me to a career I love, and giving me a solid base in grooming basics. I also met Beth through their internship program. In addition, I credit them with pissing me off enough to put a deposit down on a mobile grooming van in 2001 at Groom Expo.

There was little to no education particular to mobile grooming in those days and experience was the best teacher. I made a ton of mistakes. But I learned from each and every one of them.

This book is a labor of love and represents, between Beth and I, a cumulative experience of 45+ years.

This book could not have been written without encouragement and opportunities.

First I would like to thank my husband, Ernesto, for going with the flow all these years. Love ya!

Beth Cristiano for agreeing to not only write this book, but her unwavering confidence in whatever I throw her way.

Daryl Conner and Barbara Bird for encouragement and kindly criticisms.

Todd Shelley, Judy Breton, and Stephen Mart for all the opportunities they have offered me over the years.

And to the ladies of The Kitchen Table. You know who you are.

From Beth

For me it started in a Yonkers, NY shop back in 92' where I was officially introduced to professional pet grooming. It was love at first sight! Through much blood, (mostly my own), sweat, and tears, I found a way to love what I do and do what I love. I am grateful for the kind and generous people sent to me on this journey

Glenna and Val, thank you for teaching me the art of grooming. "A good groomer will never go hungry."

The nationally-branded company who was great for learning both how-to and how-not-to run the business side of things.

Mary, glad I can count on you to poke me forward and for not accepting status quo.

Craig, my love, thank you for your unwavering devotion and for teaching me how to "just" be.

Mom, from when I was a child, you encouraged me to dream big. You empowered me with the tools needed to be a self-sufficient, educated woman and have ALWAYS been my biggest cheerleader.

Billy, thanks for the gifts of critical thinking and the mechanical education needed to fix just about anything.

My staff, throughout the years each one of you have touched my life and continue to teach me valuable lessons that can not be gleaned from any text or class.

I thank you all for making me the person I am today and for shaping who I may become tomorrow.

1

Start Your Business

GOAL:
Find quality-building materials
to begin construction of your
business.

"There are no secrets to success. It is the result of preparation, hard work, and learning from failure."

~ Colin Powell

Are You Sure You Want to Do This?

The truth of the matter is not everyone is suited to mobile grooming. You are on your own, without the camaraderie of a shop. Traffic and school buses can be the bane of your existence. It's way too easy to run into the gas station while filling up and grabbing junk to eat. Mechanical failure can leave you on the side of the road. The list can go on and on. But for those of us that love mobile grooming, there is simply no alternative.

Before you spend a lot of money and get into debt over a vehicle, spend some time with a mobile groomer. Do a ride along. Do it more than once. You will run into one of two types of mobile groomers when you start asking around. One type will shun you and the other will welcome you with open arms. Fortunately, there are more of the welcoming types around. Network with them.

Join a couple of mobile grooming forums on Facebook. There is a wealth of information and experience at the tip of your fingers. Perhaps see if you can find a reputable mobile groomer to consult with for a fee. The more information you have, the better educated your decision will be.

In short, do your homework.

Research

Do Your Research

Resources abound for the budding entrepreneur.

The Small Business Administration (SBA) is a wealth of information regarding everything you need to know about starting a business. At time of print, there are 61 online programs and 29 guides. In addition, every state has its own chapter. www.sba.gov.

State Economic Resource Centers are designed to help a small business stay compliant with particular state rules and regulations. The SBA has conveniently compiled a list of local resources by state. www.sba.gov/tools/local-assistance/wbc.

The Department of Labor (DOL) has both federal and state divisions, which are helpful if you plan to have employees. It is imperative you consult both federal and state to see what is expected of you as an employer. They can provide much information to help you navigate hiring, maintaining, and terminating a workforce. You will have to look up your state's Department of Labor website. Federal Department of Labor: www.dol.gov.

The Occupational Safety and Health Administration, or "OSHA," is part of the federal department of labor. Its primary focus is safety in the workplace. They, too, offer safety and compliance workshops as well as site visits to ensure you are following federal guidelines in your workplace. Their suggestions help to reduce workplace injuries and increase overall safety awareness. www.osha.com.

A DOT registration number is required in some states. Check with the local Department of Motor Vehicles to find out if your state requires it for mobile grooming vans and trailers.

SCORE, counselors to America's small businesses, offers one-on-one mentoring. They also offer a library of online and onsite business programs and a library of business materials. www.score.org.

Local regulations may be particular pertaining to business in your area. Many municipalities have economic development offices. If not, start with the zoning department.

Online business programs such as marketing, planning, and accounting, are widely available online. One such resource is **www.PawsitiveEd.com**.

Get a business coach. Ask for recommendations. A business coach will help you navigate getting a business up and running. While you will eventually learn all you need, a business coach can deliver that information sooner, so you can avoid learning things the hard way.

Home Owner Associations (HOA), apartment buildings, and even personal residences often have regulations regarding parking commercial vehicles. This includes personal cars with lettering. In addition, they may not have the necessary electrical or water hooks up available. A Google search for local commercial parking rentals will bring up their availability.

Chambers of Commerce are associations made up of local business owners. They may offer local business programs.

Water and electrical hook ups are often needed for mobile vans and trailers. Needs vary amongst different parts of the country. Colder regions would benefit from indoor water lines, and interior water fills to prevent freezing of water lines. Separate waterproof electrical hook ups are also beneficial.

Research now will prevent headaches, problems and possible fines down the line.

Putting It on Paper

Write down your plan. For some us it may be a PDF on your computer, others on paper. Whichever you are more comfortable with. Writing out business plans, choosing your name, and cataloging your strengths and weaknesses are the blueprint for your business. Just as a builder would never construct a home without a blueprint, a business needs one as well. Referring to it when you hit a snag will make it easier to make adjustments and keep you on track.

Business Name

There are 3.5 billion Google searches everyday by people looking to solve a problem or looking for local services. The name of a business should be easy to remember, easy to spell, and clear in intention.

Easy to remember means brief, to the point, and meaningful. Cutesy spellings, are not always easy to remember, and autocorrect may change it to the non-cutesy version during a Google search. If a potential client has to guess what you offer, you may be passed over.

> Bad example:
> "Pretty Pawz On Your Doorstep"

Why? Because "Pretty Paws" is a common grooming name and autocorrect will change it to your potential competitors name. Because it's an uncommon spelling, a client may not remember the "Z." The name lacks clarity.

Just because we know what we mean, doesn't mean a potential client does.

Better example:
"Pretty Paws Mobile Grooming"

Even better:
"Pretty Paws Mobile (Dog) (Cat) (Pet) Grooming"

SWOT Analysis

SWOT stands for Strengths, Weaknesses, Opportunities, and Threats.

Take a piece of paper and divide it into four sections. Each square is labeled with Strength, Weakness, Opportunity, and Threats respectively.

Strengths

What are you good at? Do you have an area of expertise that would attract clients? This may include specialty trims, hand stripping, cat grooming, or handling special needs pets. Not sure what your strong suits are? Ask your current clients what they love about you. A marketing strategy should capitalize on grooming strengths. This would be a good time to do a client survey. More on surveys in Listen To Your Business chapter.

What about business skills? They are as important as your grooming abilities. Are you social media savvy? Love accounting? Are you very organized? Jot them all down as nothing is insignificant. This is not the space to be humble.

Weaknesses

This can be something you need help with or simply you don't want to do. Weaknesses need to be addressed. If not, they can become threats.

In the beginning, weaknesses will far outweigh strengths. However, you can turn any weakness into strength with education or smart hiring. It won't be long before strength surpasses weaknesses.

Opportunities

Is your local Chamber of Commerce offering free business classes? Maybe the shop down the street is thinking of selling their business. You catch the "mobile grooming van for sale ad" as its being posted. Opportunities require you to pay attention and act upon them. If you think too long, they may pass you by. To take advantage of such opportunities, you need to be prepared to act as soon as possible. Take the action. Do the work. While it appears that every successful person simply had their success handed to them, in reality that is not the case. They took the action and did the work.

Threats

This is not just worrying about the competition. Threats can also be zoning, local regulations, changes to regulations, and neglected repairs that can pose a problem. What weaknesses have you left unresolved that are now negatively impacting your business? Detailing all possible threats may help to reduce their impact as it gives you time to deal with those issues.

A SWOT analysis is good place to see how ready you are or if you need to work on some skills. Redo the SWOT analysis every year, as this is a fluid document. Circumstances can change from year to year and a SWOT analysis can help you navigate them.

Business Plan

A business plan will have everything you need to know about your business right at your fingertips. It is an invaluable tool to propel your business ever onwards and upward. A basic plan has seven sections:

1. **Business Description**—What does your business do? How do you deliver it? What makes you qualified? What is your why? Your why is the reason you get out of bed in the morning to go to work. What do you love about your business? This is more than the name of your business and your core service or product. Let the soul of your business shine through. Don't be shy.

2. **Products and Services**—Detailed descriptions of all your services and products, including what makes them unique. This section should include how you decided on pricing, as well as time spent delivering the product or service. After all, time is money. Does your pricing reflect your operating costs?

3. **Sales and Marketing Strategies**—How are you acquiring your clients? This section should detail all forms of marketing, including your website and social media. The most important part is the metrics of past strategies; what worked and what did not. Meaning, which strategies netted you

clients? If you are just getting started, this section would detail your upcoming marketing plans.

4. **Day-to-Day Operations**—What does it take to run your business? This includes overhead, start-up costs, employees, outside support professionals, salary (yours), and endgame. Unless you plan on working until the day you die, you must plan for the end of your business. That's retirement and/or the sale of your business. Your business will command a higher price if you can demonstrate its value through documentation, such as yearly updated business plans and tax returns. Your outside business support personnel may include accountants, marketers, lawyers, service repair technicians, insurance agents, coaches, suppliers, and so forth.

5. **Development**—While every other section is based on facts, here is where you can dream. What are you planning to offer in the future? This holds space for you make those plans.

6. **Financial Summary**—If you have not started your business, then your income is projected based on similar businesses. When comparing projections do it for the same month. For example: compare March of one year to March of the next. No detail is too small. Account for every penny. The health of your business depends on your familiarity with your financial summary.

Accounting software makes this easier than you think. Income should be separated and divided by everything you sell or every offered service. When you track each income stream individually, you can see what is making money and what is not. Are you allocating resources that are not adding to your bottom line? You'll know that if you track your expenses. IRS Publication 535 lists all deductible expenses. It is a good place to start if you are uncertain as to what business expenses you will have.

7. **Business Summary**—Sums up your business in easy to read bullet points. Most financial institutions, investors, or prospective buyers will read this first before making the decision to read further.

Writing these documents gives you the tools to make intelligent decisions regarding the future of your business, based on real time analysis rather than conjecture and guesswork. It adds measurable value to your business.

Vehicle Choices

Decisions, decisions, decisions. There are many options when it comes to your vehicle of choice. Be sure to check the Resource section of the book for handy links.

House Call

This might seem to be a simple choice. Just use your personal car. However, a house call groomer hauls all grooming equipment in the vehicle from location to location. Time is money. Can you easily and quickly remove equipment from the car and bring into the home? Storage and portability needs to be taken into consideration. In densely populated urban areas, cars are not convenient. A house-call groomer may need a different type of vehicle, namely; the train or bus. Using public transportation will impact equipment necessities. In addition, your equipment may be dependent upon the available amperage in your client's home. Most residential outlets are 15 amp and may have other draws on the outlet that you may be unaware of, as well as restrictive bathing and setting up areas. Ask questions regarding layout before you get to their home.

If you are using a personal vehicle for your business, your insurance agent or company needs to know that. Most likely they will add a nominal surcharge. However, better to pay the surcharge than be denied a claim because your insurance company does not cover commercial claims.

Trailer

A trailer is a stand-alone unit that is hitched to a vehicle. Trailers are heavy and the vehicle needs to be capable of carrying the extra weight. Transmission and engine size are important as you can blow out either if they are not designed for hauling. A dealership would be able to determine if you can or cannot hitch a grooming trailer safely. Driving a vehicle with a trailer attached is different than driving a car. Practice in an empty parking lot before taking it on the road. Check local driving schools to see if they offer lessons if you are not familiar with driving with a trailer attached. Some states have specific laws regarding driving with trailers. http://drivinglaws. aaa.com/tag/trailer-towing/.

The major benefit to this setup is, should you encounter vehicular malfunction you can just rent an appropriate vehicle and be back in business, minimizing down-time.

Van

A mobile grooming van is a self-contained shop on wheels. Although sometimes thought to be the most expensive option, if you do an actual cost analysis, they can be extremely cost effective.

"Vans hold their value well. When I sold my 14-year-old unit I was able to recover roughly 43% of the original purchase price." ~ Beth

Franchising

A franchise is a business model in which the owners sell the rights to their business logo, name, and model to independent operators. The largest franchise in the world is McDonald's. Franchises should be turn-key businesses with operation systems and supply routes in place. One reason people purchase franchises is because of the name\brand and what it means to consumers. If brand recognition is lacking, though, administrative support ought to be stellar to warrant buying into the franchise. The business is yours, but you still have to deal with the franchise and abide by their rules and regulations. There is no complete autonomy with a franchise.

Be sure to do your homework with this business type and fully understand the breadth of all contracts. You should work closely with your attorney and allow them to guide you through this process.

You can buy your vehicle:

- New—More expensive, but under warranty.

- Used—Less expensive, but may be subject to out-of-pocket repairs.

- Do-It-Yourself—Requires extensive mechanical skills.

Other considerations in determining which vehicle to go with is how it handles in poor weather conditions.

Most vans, Sprinters, and pickup trucks will be Rear Wheel Drive and may be tough to drive in slick road conditions. SUV's, pickups, and some newer Sprinters and vans are All Wheel Drive, which handle better in all road conditions than the Rear Wheel Drive models. SUV's, pick-ups, and Sprinters that are 4WD handle well in rough road conditions. When choosing a vehicle, make sure you know which type you are buying. Not all options are available on all vehicles.

And then there is your powering system:

Inverters use a battery pack for power. Often, the engine will idle while grooming to recharge the battery pack. In addition, the battery pack needs to be charged overnight for optimal life. Diesel engines are desirable for this application as they are better designed to handle extended idle time. Today's diesel units have superior fuel economy compared to their gas counterparts. They are very quiet; maintenance efforts and costs are a fraction of a generator. They are great for small to mid-size dogs with a minimum number of large dogs. On hand necessary supplies for diesel engines include Diesel Exhaust Fluid (DEF) and distilled water for the conversion batteries.

Generators are loud and expensive to maintain. Where they shine is consistent power throughout the day. If you plan on grooming predominately large, hairy dogs, this is the way to go. Keep the correct oil for temperature conditions on hand.

Plug in to client's homes. Your equipment usage will be dependent upon the outlet power of the client. The cord may also be a trip hazard leaving you vulnerable to a lawsuit. Climate control inside this set-up may be a challenge, as heating and cooling components draw a lot of power. As you have no control over how a home owner has routed power throughout their home, you may damage an already overextended or aging line. In addition, a homeowner may not have a dedicated line with sufficient amps to power necessary equipment.

- Any combination of the above three.

Where are the water and electrical hook ups at your residence, parking facility, or garage located? If you are in colder climates, it is easiest for water hookups to be in the interior of a home or garage, and the water fill should be inside the vehicle as well. If it is not possible to have the faucet inside a building, you will need to have a plumber install a frost-free spigot. This special type of hookup will significantly decrease the chances of a frozen spout or burst pipe.

Units with inverters will need to be plugged in year-round to provide a trickle charge to the batteries. This will extend the life of the system's batteries. Units with generators will need to be plugged in for heaters during colder months. We recommend a dedicated, waterproof receptacle, installed by an electrician.

This will be the bulk of your start-up costs. Talk with other mobile groomers and get their opinions. Schedule ride-alongs in as many different units as possible. Finally, once you have a general idea of what you want, talk to mobile manufacturers to answer any remaining technical questions. Take the time to research all options before deciding what is best for you.

2

Support Your Business

GOAL:
Find quality-building materials
to begin construction of your
business.

"Great things in business are never done by one person. They're done by a team of people."

~ Steve Jobs

Support Systems

Personal Support

It's nice to have the emotional support of friends and family when making life-changing decisions, but the reality is, that's not always the case. Being a successful business owner is a state of mind. Knowing you are prepared and can demonstrate it with a written business plan and other documentation from chapter one can keep the naysayers at bay, and offer the blueprint to keep your business on track.

Networking with other professionals via social media, local business groups, and even "Meet-Ups" can offer emotional support and valuable business advice.

Facebook has several mobile grooming groups like, The Mobile Grooming Zone, Cool Mobile Groomers, and Mobile Pet Groomers Discussion. In addition, there are regional mobile grooming groups. Then add in business groups: Grooming Business Owners, Grooming Legal Resources and Discussions, The Business Side of Pet Grooming. There are the educational based groups such as Pet Groomer Town Hall, Grooming Smarter, and Pro Groomer Network. Facebook groups come and go, but there is wealth of information to be had by those more experienced and willing to share their knowledge.

Professional Support

You are not expected to know everything about everything when it comes to opening and running a business. There are professionals who can help. The key word here is professional. Anytime you think you can save some money by doing it yourself, remember all the grooms you fixed because a pet owner wanted to save some money.

Professionals You May Need

Certified Public Accountant—set up quarterly tax schedules, year-end tax, as well as month-to-month financials, if needed. Both federal and state departments of revenue will fine and collect interest if you do not file quarterly tax payments if you fall outside their acceptable percentage of total amount due.

Banker—familiar with your business on a personal level.

Business Coach—can help navigate and guide you on how to run a business.

Business Lawyer—filing business structure with correct municipalities.

Electrician—installs dedicated electrical lines and water-proof receptacle according to building code.

Graphic Designer—for unique and personal logo and branding materials

Insurance Agent—familiar with the particulars of the mobile grooming industry. We recommend pet industry specific agencies as they are familiar with the needs of our industry. Insurance companies will break up our insurance into two policies. One for the vehicle and the other for business. If they are not linked, you run the risk of your business policy only being in effect in your driveway.

Mechanic—your business does not make money if your vehicle is sitting in a repair shop waiting to be fixed. A good relationship with a vehicle, generator, conversion mechanic is a must.

Plumber—installing water lines specific to your fill up needs.

Social Media Marketer—this is an overfilled industry. However, a good social media manager is worth their weight in gold.

Trademark Attorney. This is a specialty. If your name is sufficiently different you can prevent others from using it. However, it is expensive and time consuming, and if not done correctly, will be denied. Mary's regret is not trademarking "Pawsitively Pretty" back in 2002. Her current trademark took 8 months and $800 through a trademark lawyer.

Website Designer—also an overfilled industry. You need a well-designed, correctly Search Engine Optimized (SEO) website in today's market.

You may not need everyone on this list, but remember that to fix problems down the line will cost more in lost business, revenue, and possibly fines. Take the time to interview more than one applicant for each position. Be sure you find them to be knowledgeable and approachable. You can have "the best" lawyer in the region but they are of no use if you feel you can't talk to them. Also, make sure they talk to you like the professional you are. Just because you are not a mechanic does not mean your service provider shouldn't explain the mechanical status of your unit.

Continuing Your Education

Can you imagine grooming a Doodle with one of these things?

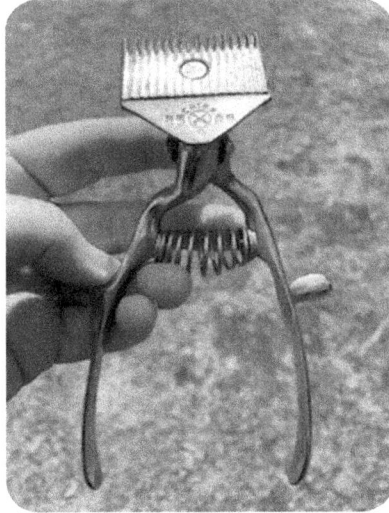

Continuing education expands our skills. Not just grooming skills, but personal development, and business expertise. There are many ways to accomplish this:

Go to trade shows. Vendors have the latest products and equipment to try out. Many booths offer free demonstrations by industry leaders. Seminars cover every aspect of grooming from breed skills to business management and everything in between. The cost of going to a trade show at least once a year should be factored into your operating costs. For a listing of upcoming trade shows: http://petgroomermagazine.com/category/ calendar/trade-shows/.

Online workshops make it easy to learn without leaving your home. Most are recorded to watch when it is convenient for you.

www.groomingprofessors.com

www.learn2groomdogs.com

www.PawsitiveEd.com

http://petgroomermagazine.com/category/ education/

Physical books are especially useful for grooming tutorials and pictures. They can be left in the grooming units for quick reference. While E-books take up less room, they may be dependent on cellular or Wi-Fi signal.

Magazine trade publications contain a wealth of information and keep you apprised of upcoming events. Subscriptions are often free, making them very economical. If you are concerned about staying green, pass them along to another who may benefit or subscribe online.

Professional associations offer the opportunity to become certified in grooming skills through a combination of educational manuals, on site and online programing, and skills testing is available at most trade shows.

Nothing beats the live and in-person experience. This can be achieved by seeking a seasoned professional to mentor you. Or mentor someone yourself as there is a lot to learn from a mentee seeing something from a fresh perspective. Some educators will travel to you: just gather a group of colleagues or collaborate with other local business owners to have enough heads to meet any minimums the instructor may have.

Let's not forget that there are numerous studies that conclude the more on-going education you receive, the higher your income tends to be.

Supporting Materials

Support materials form the basis of your marketing plan. This is not the movies where "if you build it, they will come." A solid plan includes physical materials to hand out to potential clients.

Business Cards

Money spent on business cards is a poor business decision if they end up in the garbage can. Some do's and don'ts:

Do use a photo. Professionally done head shot photos add a personal touch. Even better is to use one of you grooming a pet.

Do use larger fonts. If clients have to pull out the magnifying glass to read your card, it will be tossed. Keep font size anywhere between 10 and 14 point depending on style of fonts. Use larger fonts for headings and smaller fonts for supporting information.

Do use readable fonts. Script looks fancy, but can be tough to decipher. A potential client will not spend time trying to figure out the name of your business, phone number, website, or email. Mixing font types on business cards is okay as long as they are complementary to each other. Not sure what to use? Google "font pairs" and several sites will come up to help you make a decision. The same thing goes for colors.

https://color.adobe.com/create/color-wheel is a great start to choosing complementary or contrasting colors. It includes the hex codes to input to sites such as Canva when creating your own cards. A hex code is a 6-digit alphanumeric code that is particular to any given shade. Be consistent with colors, as even similar shades are noticeably different in print.

Don't include too much information. Keep it brief in easy-to-read bullet points. You want the person to remember what you do at a glance.

Don't be vague. You don't want a client to guess what service you are offering. Be precise in the services you offer and area you serve. Do you have a specialty, such as geriatric handling, hand stripping, or breed specific trims? Let potential clients know how you can help them.

Don't use Gmail or Hotmail email addresses. It gives the impression you are not serious about your business. After all, if you won't pony up for a legitimate website, then how important is your business? You don't want potential clients to wonder if you will still be in business a year from now. In addition, free email servers are routinely hacked. You wouldn't want clients to get a phishing email from "you."

Don't use light text on light backgrounds or dark text on dark backgrounds. Numerous studies indicate that darker text on light backgrounds work best.

Do not use your home printer. Text and photos may be blurry and not centered well. Most printer inks will bleed if they get wet. Nothing says you cut corners or are unprepared like sloppy looking business cards.

Don't use the popular designs found at Vistaprint. If you decide to use their templates, start on page four. Or you can upload your own logo and designs.

Do you know what is better than plain old paper business cards? Magnetic business cards. No one ever throws them out and you can stick them directly onto the van so people passing by can just take them. You can still keep paper business cards on the outside of your vehicle with a magnetic business card holder.

Don't use business cards as a crutch. Talk to people. The reason 90% of business cards end up in the trash is because people don't remember why they took the card in the first place.

Brochures

You can add more detailed information in a brochure, but all the rules of a business card still apply here. Keep paragraphs to no more than three sentences and use bullet points for easy readability.

Event Materials

Once the weather warms up, most communities host a series of outdoor events and fairs, animal shelters, pet fairs, craft fairs, health and wellness expos to name but a few. The American Pet Products Association estimates that 7 out 10 families own a pet, any event will have 70% of their attendees who are potential clients.

You will need:

- Six-foot folding table.

- Nice covering for said table.

- Chair

- Pop-up tent. The sun will be brutal outdoors for 6 hours.

Donuts

Donuts with your business cards and brochures to be handed out at vet offices, to be more specific. Once you walk in with the box of donuts you will have everyone's attention while they eat and you extoll the virtues of your business.

Order smaller quantities of printed materials. It's better to re-order multiple times than throw out unused cards because you wanted to change things up or phone numbers change.

Don't forget other business's newsletters. Offer to write a pet tip article for their clients in exchange for putting your contact information in their newsletter. Suggestions include: veterinarians, pet stores, weekly local publications, breed/agility clubs, high-end home-owner's associations, and golf clubs.

Retirement

You haven't even started mobile grooming and we're talking about retirement. The earlier you plan for your retirement, the better off you will be. Unless of course, you plan to work up until the day they bury you.

Many folks foolishly do not plan for retirement. And those who have a plan may not know how to execute it. Unfortunately, that is still not enough. You will need to determine when you will retire, how you want to live, and how much you will need to live that way.

There are two ways to plan. The first is through savings, 401K, IRA's, stock and so forth. This is a discussion to have with your financial advisor, not two groomers.

The second is based on the resale value of your van or business. This value will hinge on how you well you maintain your vehicle and paperwork.

You should retain ALL documents, warranties, repairs and maintenance receipts. In short, you should keep every scrap of paper or digital (memo) related to your unit(s). Not only does it increase resale value it shows you are a diligent business person and will give you more weight when negotiating a fair price.

This includes keeping accurate bookkeeping records. Not only is creative bookkeeping illegal, it will not serve you well when trying to get a fair price for any part of your business.

3

Control Your Business

GOAL:
Make decisions to protect your
business and honor the direction
you envision.

"A passionate belief in your business and personal objectives can make all the difference between success and failure. If you aren't proud of what you're doing, why should anybody else be?"

~ Richard Branson

Setting Client Expectations and Boundaries

How often do we hear about clients walking all over groomers and expecting miracles? The groomer allows this, but how do you set client boundaries?

The first step is to look professional. Greet the client, including the pet with neat hair and clean, appropriate clothing. Be aware of your body language. Stand straight without leaning in any direction and offer your hand, along with eye contact and a smile. It's perfectly fine to greet long-term clients with a hug. Attention is always on the client in front of you. The purpose of looking professional is for your clients to have confidence in you. Observe other professionals and how they interact with you when you are in their place of business. How do they make you feel?

Act the professional. It is your job to ensure the client is aware of your policies and procedures. You are responsible for providing clear communication. It is not the job of the owner to interpret what you mean. Any written instructions should be legible to prevent miscommunication. Ask for and provide pictures, they are worth 1,000 words. Have a portfolio of different breeds and styles available to show an indecisive client. When you complete each new groom, take a picture and send it to a dedicated email box for client pictures. Be sure to use the pet's name and groom date in the subject line. All staff members should have access to this account so they can see past grooms and update as needed.

Be the professional. While looking and acting the part offers visual cues to the client, being professional is a mindset. This is confidence in your skills and in yourself, so that when you inform your clients what needs to be done, it is accepted rather than questioned.

But where do unreasonable expectations come from?

Not setting boundaries—Allowing the client to tell you what you will do, when the pet will be ready, how much they'll pay, be chronically late or no-show, and consistently rescheduling to name a few. This is where written policies and procedures need implementation and consistent enforcement. Compile a list of common policies you want every client to know and create a "Terms of Service Agreement." Filling out this document at check-in opens the lines of communication between groomer and client while organizing important information. The service agreement must be signed and kept on file.

Guiding every client through this document section-by-section helps them to understand what you expect from them as your client and what you will provide as their pet's groomer. This is a common business practice. You sign similar documents at the doctor's office or at a child's school. It is a professional act in and of itself and can set you apart from the competition.

Under-promise, over-deliver—Help your clients realistically manage their expectations. It is not feasible to take a severely matted dog and turn him into a fluff ball. Use the word "naked" to describe what the matted pet is going to look like. Never agree to "try my best" because when an owner hears that they are envisioning a fluffy pet and will be disappointed because of your perceived promise. You over-promised and under-delivered. Conversely, if they expect "naked" and you were able to wet shave and finish with a 5—you are a hero. In this scenario, you under-promised and over-delivered. Huge difference.

Abstain from judgmental opinions—We are not privy to other people's personal life. Maybe they are uncaring owners, but what if they are dealing with a sick child, a loss of job, or any number of other personal issues? (None of which is our business.) Assume all new clients are uninformed or misinformed. As pet professionals, it is our job to educate clients. Educating them usually forms a lasting bond of respect and trust with a new client. If you cannot deliver what they want, give them options. People like options because it gives them a sense of control. A matted dog always gets three options:

   a. We can shave it naked and start over.

b. Show them how to brush and comb and reschedule so they have an opportunity to de-mat their own dog.

"I have this to be a frequently chosen option. First, they try and are unable. Then, they come back with a newfound understanding and respect for what we do." ~ Mary

This pet usually ends up on a more frequent grooming schedule as well.

c. Quote them the hourly de-matting price and the approximate time it will take, when humanely possible.

Lack of communication—There are times when we make a promise to a client in good faith, only to realize that it is not possible. This usually involves a shave down. If the style has significantly changed, do not proceed without client approval. A preferred method for obtaining approval is by text, as you will have a documented authorization to proceed. Phone approval can lead to a he-said-she-said type of situation.

There are clients that, no matter how professional you are, will never be happy and are often vocal about it. Unfortunately, some clients will need to be dismissed. For example, chronic rule breakers, those that use abusive or foul language, or exhibit inappropriate or sexual behavior.

A note on inappropriate behavior: an elderly client that suddenly engages in such behavior may be indicative of an underlying medical condition, which should be brought to the attention of their family members.

Setting and sticking to your written policies and procedures, leads to better behaved clients who are more respectful of this profession.

Pricing and Number of Pets Needed

Fair pricing is vital to your business, its employees, and clients. Money is the life-blood of running a business. One can run the most organized, well-respected business and still fail if not properly priced. Without fair pricing the business can't stay afloat nor can it properly compensate operations staff. If not properly compensated, staff, including the owner, can burn-out. Morale will suffer and some may seek other employment opportunities. Many mobile businesses have come and gone due to inadequate pricing.

Figuring out your price structure should not be a random act. It is not recommended to base your pricing solely by surveying the competition. They may not offer the same quality or type of service. Furthermore, they may have randomly chosen their prices or worse have not had an increase since opening 10 years ago.

Your pricing should be rooted in a simple process you understand and can quickly convey to others. Hourly rates are an easy way to go. They are straight forward and easy to explain to staff and clients. Hourly rates compensate for all time spent on the process. Hourly rates fairly charge the client. Why should a 2-week Yorkie be charged the same price as an 8-10-week Yorkie? They should not. Hourly rates level the playing field for all players.

The possibilities are endless. You can charge however makes sense to you as long as it is based on mathematics that reflect your expenses and income. Income must be factored into the equation. Without it you have an incomplete figure that will force you to supplement your business, whether it be with time or money. If you do not account for a reasonable salary then you have a hobby, NOT a business.

Determining how many pets are needed begins with determining how much to charge. This is decided by how much is needed to run your business and make a living. Cost of living is different from one region to another, as are lifestyle choices.

Add up all projected business expenses over the course of a year. Refer to IRS Publication 587 to be as complete as possible. Then add your desired annual income. Decide how many weeks out of 52 you plan to work. Please take time for vacation. Divide yearly expenses and income by the number of working weeks. That yields the weekly gross amount required.

The Formula:

$$\frac{(annual)\ expenses\ +\ income}{number\ of\ weeks\ worked} = \begin{array}{l} amount\ needed\ each\ week \\ (a.k.a.\ weekly\ gross\ target) \end{array}$$

Your number of pets:

As an example, we will use $2,000 a week based on a 48-week year and three common price points at the time this book was printed: $65, $75, and $85 an hour.

The Formula:

$$\frac{weekly\ gross\ target}{hourly\ or\ average\ ticket\ charge} = number\ of\ pets\ needed$$

To gross $2000 a week based on one hour or less grooms

$65/hr. = 31 pets
$75/hr. = 27 pets
$85/hr. = 24 pets

Number of clients needed on a 6-week schedule:

$65 = 186 pets
$75 = 162 pets
$85 = 144 pets

Let's tweak that number for 4 vs. 8 week pets:

4-week			8-week
$65	124	vs.	248
$75	108	vs.	216
$85	96	vs.	192

You can see a huge difference in the number of pets you need based on amount and frequency.

Charging more allows you work at an easier pace with less stress on your body. Having clients commit to a more frequent schedule keeps the pets in more manageable coats reducing wear and tear on you and your equipment, as well as encouraging a pleasant experience for all. In addition, it keeps income stable.

You may notice these figures are based on a 48 not 52-week year. That's because we account for vacation time. We recommend scheduling vacation from the start. Otherwise, you will get busy, making it harder and harder to take time off.

More reasons to take vacation time:

- Stress reduction.

- Increased productivity. This is a direct result of being happier and more focused.

- Sleep better. When you stop the chatter from the responsibilities of your job and social media, your brain has an opportunity to reset itself.

And when we say vacation time, we mean leave your computer at home and limit the phone usage to taking photographs and mapping directions.

Routing and Scheduling

Like spaghetti and meatballs, chips and dips, and popcorn and movies, routing and scheduling go hand in hand. To be effective with either, both are taken into account.

Scheduling

"When I first went mobile in 2002, my father was ill and I needed flexibility as his doctor's appointments were random and usually within three weeks. What worked for me was to move ahead the client in my schedule book, but not give the next appointment. Then two weeks prior, when I knew what days my father needed to be taken to his doctors, I would route it out and let them know. I found what would cut down on no-shows was a text reminder that I was getting ready to route the week. If my clients had any pressing engagements, they could tell me then. I loved the flexibility. Yes, it's a little more work, but it allows me to take time off for unscheduled trips to visit my grandkids at the drop of a hat." ~ Mary

So now you know what Mary prefers, other options include setting the next appointment before you leave their home or get out a calendar for the upcoming year and book them throughout. The longer you set appointments out, the more they will need to be reminded. Be clear on your cancellation and no-show policy. There are apps and software that will send automatic reminders.

Routing

If you don't think you can make a living in your area, then stick a pin in a map and draw a 30-mile radius. Pick a better area. You can always refine your service area down the road. However, it is best to start off with a focused service area before accepting clients. This leads to minimizing unnecessary drive time and eventually having to let that loyal client go that lives where you no longer serve.

All the ways you can route your schedule:

- By neighborhood

- Town

- Start at the furthest point from your home and work your way back

- Groom your way to the furthest house then groom your way home.

- Need to walk your dogs mid-day? Be in the area at that time.

- Start early in the morning

- Work later in the evening

- Work weekends

- Don't work weekends

- Equal mix of large and smaller dogs

- Cats only days

- Multiple pet household days for multiple groomer units

How do you choose? Look at your lifestyle and make a decision. You will be hard pressed to find any group of mobile groomers agreeing on any one way. If your needs change, then make the necessary changes in the way you route and schedule.

There are many options to schedule your clients, ranging from software, online services, to an old-fashioned, appointment book. However, you decide, have a back-up. If you use software or an online service, print out two weeks. If you keep a book, take a photo of the pages. Websites can go down or you could lose your appointment book. Having a secondary means of retrieving your schedule will save your day. Consider cloud-based services such as Dropbox and Google Drive. In addition, set up an email box to which you can just send copies of your schedule. If you lose any information due to a server out-age or lost book, you will be able to reconstruct your schedule as far back as you need to.

Forms

Forms are an integral part of an organized business. They help to convey and store all sorts of information. Some common forms used in daily operations are receipts, end-of-day sales form, client information cards\forms, report cards, terms of service agreement, and various release forms such as: medical, de-matting, elderly pet etc. These papers are tools by which we can communicate a host of information to both clients and staff alike. When something is written down it is less likely the message will be distorted; such is the use for a client report card and service agreement. The exact meaning of your findings and intentions are clearly written for the client or coworkers to understand.

Most clients do not mind filling out forms. In fact, most feel it is professional and authentic to require documentation for your services. You can either ask them to complete and print forms located on your website prior to arrival or fill them out together at check-in. Either way you should always have these forms available as some clients will forget to prepare.

Companies of one to 100+ benefit from forms. No one can be expected to remember everything. Forms help take the guess work out of your job and cover your tracks should a client complain or ask for changes to the services their pet receives. Forms can be catalogued, photographed, or scanned and stored in a file box, binder, database, cloud, or email server when needed for future reference.

We have compiled a library of forms, waivers, and checklists. They can be downloaded from:

www.PawsitiveEd.com/mobile-groomers-bible-resources/

Mobile Groomer Vehicle Safety

We depend on our vehicles in order to make a living. We can reduce the likelihood of our businesses being down due to mechanical failure or body repair by being familiar with their capabilities and limitations.

Let's start with dimensions.

Know the height of your vehicle before going through drive-thrus, entering parking garages, and driving under low bridges. When measuring height, do so when tires are set at the correct pressure. The difference between low and proper tire pressure could be several inches. Don't trust whoever did the measuring on bridges, drive thrus, and such, subtract about 4 inches from posted measurements.

Width and length determines whether you can turn around in a driveway or need to back in. It can be tough to see oncoming traffic when backing out of a driveway. Trailers may be disengaged from the car and manually turned around.

Sit in the driver's seat and have someone walk around your vehicle and note where you lose sight of him or her. Install extra mirrors and backup cameras to compensate. Use both when backing up and note low hanging branches and wires, as well as basketball hoops and mailboxes. In addition, check the condition of the driveway. Are there wet leaves or black ice? Both are equally dangerous. Are bushes blocking your view of the road? Have kids left their toys on the driveway?

"I have had to be towed to the repair shop because I ran over a kid's scooter that managed to pull out my heater hoses." ~ Mary

Never allow someone else to direct you. They frequently do not take your height, weight or lack of flexibility into account. There are countless stories of groomers that had accidents due to a "helpful" eye. It is your vehicle and your responsibility to safely maneuver it.

Remember learning how to drive? Most of us were taken to an empty parking lot to get a feel for the car before taking it out on the open road. It is recommended to rent a van, truck, or trailer of comparable size before you get behind the wheel of your expensive and difficult-to-replace grooming unit. It gives you a low-pressure opportunity to get intimately acquainted with your vehicle. The parking lot introduction is suggested for all people, staff or buyers who will be driving.

Don't forget these units are heavy! They weigh significantly more than the average car plus they are hauling our equipment and hundreds of pounds of water. This means we cannot stop on a dime, and can sink into soggy spots. It is imperative to recognize this. You must leave plenty of room... more than usual between you and the car in front. Folks do not like to get stuck behind us so they frequently zoom ahead and cut us off. As earlier mentioned, we can't stop quickly, so drive defensively.

Weather

Even if you can drive just fine in whatever Mother Nature throws your way, consider the driving skills of others. Totaled is totaled, no matter who is at fault. There are no mobile grooming van rentals available while we wait for the vehicle to be repaired. Take high wind alerts seriously. There is a lot of empty air space in trailers and vans. High winds can push your vehicle over into oncoming traffic or adjacent vehicles. A question to ask yourself before you head out in poor weather or road conditions is: "If I get into an accident, will this groom even cover my deductible?"

Roads

Watch those potholes. They can damage suspension and throw engine computers out of whack. Scenic roads, AKA dirt roads, can rattle everything loose and, if muddy, can result in a tow job. Pay attention to other drivers. Secure all equipment and supplies. Stopping short will send everything flying resulting in damage.

Maintenance

Check tire pressure regularly. Low tire pressure impacts fuel consumption, and can cause hydroplaning on slick roads. Use the manufacturer recommended tires and follow the rotation schedule. Cheaper tires will wear faster, and may reduce stopping power.

Schedule maintenance per manufacturer recommendations. For some scheduled maintenance, it is wise to have the service done a bit sooner than recommended. Service intervals are usually based on miles. Those who idle all day with inverters are racking up engine hours. To off-set the difference, pre-emptively schedule appointments. It will keep your vehicle in top shape and establish a relationship with your mechanic. This relationship is important if you need a quick appointment. Include periodic brake line and exhaust leak checks. Most mechanical breakdowns can be prevented with regular maintenance.

No matter how diligent we are with maintenance, break-downs will happen. It is important to know what type of tow truck is recommended for your unit and whether it should be towed from the front, rear, or on a flatbed.

Hook Ups

We mean electrical and water. Protect electrical hookups from moisture by properly storing all cords and installing waterproof covers and receptacles. Before leaving any residence, including your own, walk around the vehicle. Make sure all lines are disengaged and doors are closed.

Detectors

We need three of them.

1. **Fire/smoke detector**—Plus add a fully charged, securely mounted fire extinguisher.

   "I cannot emphasize the words securely mounted. It is

a sight to behold a fire extinguisher spraying foam all over your van. It is mess to clean up and you might as well toss any blades or scissors that get caught up in the foam." ~ Mary

2. **Carbon monoxide detector**—This can save your life. Carbon monoxide is odorless and by the time symptoms present, the damage is done. Carbon monoxide can seep into your work area through exhaust leaks, generator exhaust, or even lawn crews working near your vehicle.

"I could not understand why I began to be so cranky at work. Wonderful pets became agitated and difficult to work with. After talking it over with a colleague we realized my exhaust was recycled into the work area, poisoning me. I immediately installed a detector and extended the tail pipe. Problem solved. Happy days were here again." - Beth

3. **Your nose**—While propane is odorless, a substance is added to propane so you can smell it.

*Special note for trailers: Transmission and engine size matter. If you are not certain, talk to the dealership's repair shop for safety information. Use a matching ball and tongue and utilize the chains and pin. Check all connections at each stop. If you have never driven a trailer before, rent a Uhaul and practice, practice, practice in a parking lot before buying.

We don't make money when our vehicles are in the

parking lot of a repair facility, waiting to be fixed. Add in the inconvenience to our clients, and you can see why being familiar with our vehicles, keeping up the maintenance, and buying quality parts will pay off in the long run.

Pet Safety

We are responsible for the pets in our care. Their safety is paramount. The client has entrusted their beloved furry family members into our care. It is our responsibility to keep them safe from beginning to end. An injured pet is more than just an injury. It can result in pain for the pet, loss of that client, a social media nightmare, and/or veterinarian reimbursement.

All pets should be in your control. That's means using your slip lead for dogs. Most collars are too loose and a dog could easily slip out and run off. Put cats in your hard-shelled carrier. You know the condition of your personal carrier. Owner carriers that are broken or held together with bread ties are at risk for breakage while bringing the cat out to your van.

Take your time and don't rush the pet or yourself. Give the pet a chance to acclimate to your vehicle. Accidents are more likely to happen when you are trying to quickly finish up a pet.

Always note what products are used on each pet. We recommend using products that list full ingredients. If the groomer or the pet has a reaction, you don't want to play 20 questions with the manufacturer trying to figure out the problem ingredient. Cat safe and dog safe claims are strictly up to the manufacturer. There is no regulatory agency overseeing that.

Know any medical conditions that may worsen under

the stress of grooming such as arthritis, allergies, diabetes, seizures, and heart conditions to name a few.

Orthopedic mats on the table, floors, and in tubs will help ease the joints of elderly pets. In the resource section is "The Old Lady Speech." It details to the owner how the needs of elderly pets are met and change over time. There is a point in which a groomer cannot safely finish the pet. The owner needs to be made aware of that fact. Always keep a hand on a blind or deaf pet so they won't be startled when you need to do something.

There is no space too small that a cat can't get through. Lock it down. Close all windows and lock the doors. Stuff a towel into any opening.

"It's no fun dismantling the dashboard of your van because a cat squeezed its way into the cab and right up into the dashboard." ~ Mary

There are some pets that are better served by being groomed at the vet. When in doubt, don't! This includes the aggressive pet that needs to be sedated, or the chronically ill pet that should be close to the vet while grooming.

Restraining an unruly pet makes it safer for both the groomer and the pet. However, it needs to be humane. (See Resources) Hip supports are great for older/arthritic dogs as it helps to relieve some of the stress on their joints while standing. But, if the pet is relying on the hip support, it can only do so safely for about 10 minutes as the hip support will compress the pet's organs and may damage nerves.

Allowing or not allowing clients in your vehicle is a personal decision as well as a conversation you should have with your insurance agent beforehand. As a general rule, and a general rule only: In most cases, a dog's behavior is made worse by the owner, whereas a cat's behavior improves.

Take a pet first aid class that incorporates the most current protocols and includes hands-on training. Take that class every two years. These skills are use or lose them. However, these skills may save the life of the pet in your care.

Circuit breakers pop. Sometimes within arms reach, but mostly they are in the back of the vehicle. Do not leave a pet unattended on the table or tub while you run around to the back of the vehicle. It takes a second for a pet to snap their neck falling or jumping. If you must leave the vehicle to reset a circuit, place the pet on the floor or in a carrier.

Precautions taken now will reduce the likelihood of pain and suffering to our clients, as well as causing loss of revenue to our businesses.

Personal Wellbeing and Safety

In order to have a lasting career as a mobile groomer, we need to take care of ourselves.

We are on our feet for most of the day. Good quality orthopedic mats are a must. Most workman's compensation claims are orthopedic in nature. These preventable injuries can result in lost revenue for businesses. On the heels of this (pun intended) is purchasing quality, closed-toed, waterproof footwear.

"There is nothing worse than wet feet with hair splinters in both." ~ Mary

Regularly changing your physical position will reduce musculoskeletal injuries. In addition to sitting for driving and standing for grooming, add a stool to sit as well. Working at the correct height is important, too. Use adjustable tables.

If any pet injures you, stop the groom, secure the pet, and attend to the injury. Your pet first aid kit should contain supplies for yourself as well.

If you have physical limitations, honor them. Not every pet needs to be groomed by you.

We suggest you wear waterproof clothing in the form of smocks and aprons. Wet clothing can lead to rashes. A change of clothing is a good idea in the event you get soaked or suspect a pet has something contagious.

It is important to have a selection of muzzles,

Elizabethan collars, and humane restraints for any pet that is a bite risk. Bites can be career ending, so take the possibility seriously.

Eat breakfast. Your body is more efficient and your mind more focused when you start the day with breakfast. Drink plenty of water. We work in dehydrating conditions. Dehydration taxes your organs and can lead to premature chronic conditions. It's healthier to bring lunch rather than stopping at a fast food joint.

For the safety of both you and the pet, there should be no distractions while working and driving. That means put the cell phones away while doing either. That said, you can use your cell phone to video record every groom. Mount the phone using a flexible tripod. You can email this video to a specific address that is just for those videos. In the event a client falsely accuses you of harming their pet, you have video proof. While most video files will be too large to upload via email, apps such as Dropbox or Google Drive should accommodate them.

A little care now will contribute to a long and fulfilling career.

Sanitation

Our work areas are so much different than a shop. Add in that we may track contagions from one yard into our vans, and then into another client's home. Because of that everything needs to be cleaned. You can reduce the workload by keeping supplies in closed containers and watching where you walk.

There is a difference between cleaning and disinfecting. Cleaning removes the most common vectors of transmission of contagions: the biological. Biologicals include hair, dander, dirt, blood, urine, and feces. Contagions are bacteria, viruses, and spores that have the potential to spread disease. Cleaners do not necessarily disinfect. Disinfecting disables the contagion, preventing cross-contamination, but disinfectants work better on clean surfaces.

Cleaning and Disinfecting Products

Undiluted 70 % Rubbing Alcohol—Rubbing alcohol is considered a solvent and dissolves dirt and oils. It is used in hospitals. Even though cats cannot metabolize alcohol, it dries almost instantly and without residue, therefore it can be used around cats once the alcohol has dried. If used as a disinfectant, the surface must remain wet for 10 minutes.

Portable Steam Cleaners—The reservoir is filled with water and the steam cleaner heats the water hot enough to produce steam. Unlike many liquid cleaners, a steam cleaner can get into porous surfaces such as grout and floor and wall seams.

50/50 Vinegar-to-Water Mix—Vinegar is mildly acidic and as such has anti-bacterial properties, however, the EPA does not list it as a disinfectant. It is Mary's cleaner of choice. Vinegar is also abrasive and breaks up dirt and oils. If you want it to smell better, then add some orange or lemon rinds to the bottle. You can add essential oils as well, but make sure any cats do not have access to those surfaces. Oils may leave a residue that can be absorbed through a cat's pads.

Hydrogen Peroxide—One cup of hydrogen peroxide to a gallon of water can be used as a cleaner. Hydrogen peroxide is listed as antibacterial and antiviral from the EPA. In order to take advantage of those disinfecting properties it must:

a. Be undiluted in the brown bottle. Once opened or used in clear containers will start the degradation process. Hydrogen peroxide will turn into water.

b. Remain on the surface for 20 minutes.

Soap—Plain old soap and water removes the biological

that may cause transmission of disease when washing our hands and rinsing down the tub in between pets.

Ultra Violet Sanitizers use UV light to sanitize tools and workspaces. When used in the manner that the manufacturer sets forth, UV light destroys micro-organisms, viruses, mold, and bacteria without dangerous chemical agents.

Norwex Microfiber Cloths—These are specially treated cloths that lift dirt instead of moving it around. They just require spraying the area first with water, then wiping with the cloth. The manufacturer makes antibacterial and antiviral claims as silver is used in the treatment process, but, we don't know how accurate that is, or for how long the cloths keep those properties. They do a great job of cleaning without the mess of paper towels, and your work area almost sparkles after using them. You cannot buy them at a store. Distributors sell them. Don't buy them on Amazon as vendors jack up the price considerably. You can find a distributor easily on Facebook by posting a request in any of the Facebook grooming groups.

Air Cleaners—To efficiently clean the air without neurochemicals, air circulation fans, plants, and salt lamps are effective. Effective air circulation needs intake and outtake fans. Plants do their thing by releasing oxygen and absorbing VOC's (volatile organic compounds). VOC's are the harsh chemicals found in paints, aerosols, and certain cleaners. Salt lamps neutralize positively charged bacteria, dust, and pollen when they are heated by lamp or candle. The heat attracts water in the air and separates the salt ions. There are now more loose negatively charged chloride ions that can bind with those positively charged bacteria in the air. That's the flaking you see on the counter around salt lamps.

Enzymatic Cleaners—These spray cleaners utilize enzymes to break down bacteria and dirt. In addition, they penetrate porous surfaces such as grout, floor and wall seams. Nature's Miracle is a highly-rated enzymatic cleaner.

Essential Oils—Essential oils such as lemon, wild orange, and eucalyptus are great for cleaning. You can find many cleaning recipes online. Essential oils will leave a residue when dried. They should not be used around cats, as cats cannot metabolize most essential oils. The latest guidelines from the National Association of Holistic Aromatherapists states that essential oils should not be used in any form around cats or birds.

Bleach—A 10% dilution of bleach to water kills everything and can damage nasal and lung linings. Also, using diluted bleach in your unit may void any or all conversion warranties. Discuss this limitation with your manufacturer. Use only as necessary and never more than 10%. It is good for mold.

Chlorohexidine (Dakil) and Quaternary Ammonium Products (Quats) are very effective disinfectants. Follow manufacturer directions precisely.

Recirculating pumps should have a water and vinegar mix run through until the water runs clear at the end of day.

Grey water tank should be dumped daily and cleaned out once a month. If you cannot remove your grey tank, RV stores have tablets you can drop into the tank to clean it.

Day-to-day cleaning is best done as natural as possible as you are exposed to these products every day. When the situation calls for it, then Quats, bleach, and chlorohexidine products should be used.

Spares

As groomers, it's been drilled into us to have spares of our equipment. As mobile groomers, the spares list grows. In addition to spare grooming equipment, we need the following:

- Fresh water pump
- Recirculating pump
- Duct, electrical, and plumbing tape
- Screwdrivers
- Hose clamps
- Drain pump
- GFCI Outlets
- Circuit breakers
- Dryer
- Motor vehicle fluids such as engine oil, anti-freeze, and windshield wiper fluid
- Motor brushes
- Hose coupling hardware
- A couple of gallons of fresh water in the event water pumps aren't working or are frozen.

- Cord to keep working if generator/invertor is acting up.

- Key. Keep a spare in your pocket or around your neck for when you lock yourself out of the vehicle. That's not an if, but a when.

- $20 for when you forget your pocketbook/wallet and need gas or something to eat.

Or anything that breaks on a regular basis particular to your vehicle

Most repairs to a grooming part of your vehicle are quick and easy if you have spares and a nominal tool kit on hand. Replacing a fresh water pump, for example, could take you 15 minutes as opposed to driving home or worse, trying to find an open RV store and rescheduling the day.

Security

"My husband was so concerned about my safety that he took a week off from work to travel with me when I first got my van. It took him that long to realize that as long as I took precautions, I was as safe in my van as I was any place else." ~ Mary

It starts with locking your doors. The many benefits include stopping people from randomly opening your door and allowing a pet to escape: neighbors, kids, owners, and bad guys. The downside is accidently locking yourself out of the vehicle because of habit. Keep a spare key handy in your pocket, around your neck, or hidden on the outside of your vehicle.

State laws will vary regarding personal protection such as tazers, pepper gel, and fire arms. Consider taking safety programs in their use as well as personal protection classes. A can of travel-size wasp spray or your "shop" dog can be deterrents as well. When spraying anything, be aware of wind direction.

GPS systems are an invaluable resource for the mobile groomer. Not only can they get us from call to call in record time while allowing for current traffic conditions, but they can also be used to locate the groomer and\or unit. Most telephones now have the capability of being tracked. This feature can be invaluable should your vehicle breakdown in unknown territory or if your family needs to find you.

GPS is also available for the vehicle. This is not the typical system most are familiar with. These systems are actually wired into the vehicle's computer. Of course, you can track these vehicles. A really useful feature is that you can receive email alerts if the vehicle is speeding or experiencing mechanical malfunction. Receiving these alerts gives you the opportunity to remotely observe your operation while ensuring the safety of fleet and staff.

Don't go anywhere you feel unsafe or afraid. When we are fearful, our body starts dumping hormones such as adrenaline, which has a distinct odor. Animals can smell the fear on us. It can put a strain on the grooming session, making it harder to groom this pet.

You are not obligated to groom anyone's pet. If you feel uneasy, make an excuse to leave. "My water pump broke at the last call, but I was in the neighborhood and wanted to let you know directly that I need to reschedule. I will call you." Then leave. Whenever inside a client's property, ensure you have a clear exit between you and the owner.

Be aware of your surroundings. Pay attention.

For those with invertors, don't idle when going in and out of homes if your vehicle is out of sight. If you need to idle, lock the doors and keep the spare key in your hand.

Leave valuables and money out of sight from anyone casually looking in a window. If you or your employees must leave client payments in the unit, secure them in a discreetly-mounted lock-box.

Payment Options

Show us the money!

There are numerous ways to collect payment:

- At time of service (our preference)

- Invoicing

- Bank-to-bank transfer

- Stamped self-addressed envelope with invoice and left on counter

Zelle or Venmo type bank-to-bank transfers are an easy way to accept electronic payments without the added expense or security concerns of credit cards. They work seamlessly with your bank and do not generate more work when it comes time to prepare for bookkeeping. A bank-to-bank transfer can be between account holders of the same bank, or even different banks. However, both institutions have to participate with the same vendor offering the service. This is an ever-growing option now offered by most major banks and many credit unions.

Cash is king, however, if you have employees you may not want them collecting cash. Do you have a safe place to keep cash in your vehicle? You can mount a small lock box or safe in an inconspicuous spot inside the van for daily deposits. We recommend emptying the stash daily.

Checks from established bank accounts with printed name and address—Have clear "Bounced Check" policies in writing. Some states have Theft of Service laws applying to bounced checks that are not made good within a reasonable time. Your local police department can advise you on that. Some banks will let you scan checks directly into your account.

Credit card machine, Square, or Paypal—They all have their fees. (Which are a tax deductible business expense.) Most states make it illegal to charge extra for those fees. Know what the rules are for your state. If you have a bank credit card machine, there are federal guidelines you must follow. The credit card machine company will let you know what to do. They also have contracts for a specified time, with penalties, if you try to leave early. Those rules don't apply to Paypal or Square because you don't get copies of the credit card information.

IRS regulations state that you must list individual clients and amounts. There are no bulk deposits allowed. For example: John Smith- $100, Jane Doe $85, and Jane Smith $150, as opposed to $335.

However you decide to collect payment, detail it in your "Terms of Service" agreement.

Going on the Go

Yes, we're going there. (Pun intended.) Having to go to the bathroom can be an issue for mobile groomers unless our mobile units are equipped with a bathroom. Those units will have a third black tank in addition to a fresh and gray. You will have to use specific paper and never flush anything other than the aforementioned paper. You can find the right type of toilet paper at RV and camping stores. You will also have to find a location to legally drain the tank. RV sites and marinas are a good place to start.

It is not always feasible to use a client's bathroom as we may be uncomfortable entering their homes or in the middle of working on a pet. Holding urine can cause health problems for women. Irritable Bowel Syndrome or just eating something that did not agree with us may necessitate immediate use of a bathroom. Whenever making a stop for food or fuel it is recommended to take a "trying turn" at the facilities.

Our tubs drain into a gray tank, which is not designed for human waste. A better option is to have a porta potty. You can buy them at any RV store or make one from a 5-gallon container. It is imperative that you dispose of any waste in the appropriate place. There may be local ordinances that must be followed to avoid fines.

Pet First Aid Kits

Every pet professional should have pet first aid training. During such training you will realize a first aid kit is not an optional item. You will use it, even if it's on yourself. They do evolve over time as new products make their way to the market. This is a suggested list, as well as how to use each item.

Activated charcoal is used to absorb ingested poisons. Any item in a kit that is intended for poisoning should NOT be used unless directed by a veterinarian. Protocols vary and what will help in one instance can cause harm in another.

Antibiotic cream for wounds—Do not use triple antibiotic if you groom cats. While it is rare, cats may have an allergy to the combination of the three ingredients. If the cat has such an allergy, it is fatal. If you use natural products, ensure there are no essential oils if you groom cats as well. The National Association of Holistic Aromatherapists have put out new guidelines that state essential oils should not be used in any form around cats.

Antihistamine and safety pin for minor allergic reactions—Look specifically for diphenhydramine gels with a liquid center. The safety pin is used to puncture the gel cap and squirt the liquid directly into the mouth of the pet. It is the fastest way for an anaphylactic pet to absorb the antihistamine. Consult a veterinarian for proper dosing. Not all pets can safely use antihistamines as it may interfere with other medications and medical conditions.

Two apps for smart phones—The first is the ASPCA's Pet Poison app. It's FREE and will dial the number for the Pet Poison Hotline. As minutes matter in a poisoning, this is invaluable if you cannot reach a local veterinarian for instructions. The second is a veterinarian locator. They are usually free. As mobile groomers are all over the place, being able to locate a veterinarian quickly can be a lifesaver.

Baking soda to absorb topical poisons or chemicals.

Band aids for you. This will probably be your most re-plenished item.

Bandanas have multiple uses. They replace triangular bandages and can be used as slings to take the weight off of an injured limb.

Expired gift cards—They are a perfect size to cushion pad injuries on larger pets. Place gauze on both sides of the card and securely wrap the cards and gauze to the paw with vet wrap. In addition, the cards can flick out bee stingers. Place the card at the base of the stinger where it meets the skin and lift up and out.

Eyewash serves double duty. It can be used to flush out both eyes and wounds.

Gauze comes in three varieties: gauze roll, gauze pads, and nonstick gauze pads. The gauze roll is wider and is good for larger wounds. The nonstick gauze is more expensive, but I will use it as the first pad on the wound and then place the cheaper gauze on top of it. The nonstick gauze will not remove the scab when it is time to replace the bandaging.

Honey packets for hypoglycemic pets—Stress, seizures, as well as an owner giving a pet too much insulin can result in low blood sugar. This is a serious condition that may result in the death of the pet. Signs include listlessness, staggering, tremors, muscle weakness, and seizures. Do not give the pet honey unless directed by a veterinarian.

Hydrogen peroxide to induce vomiting in a dog. As this is used for poisoning, consult a veterinarian first. Dosage will vary. Vomiting is not a given for poisoning. If the ingested poison is caustic, it will burn the throat on its way out. You cannot use hydrogen peroxide to induce vomiting in cats. Cats cannot metabolize hydrogen peroxide.

Ice will constrict blood flow, slow bleeding and good for people bumps and falls. Squeeze to pop and activate ice bags are available at the local pharmacy and if available, your client's freezer may be your go-to.

Liquid bandage is an asset if you know how to use it properly. Used incorrectly, it can damage surrounding tissue, as well as trap bacteria in the wound. Your veterinarian can instruct you in proper usage. I do not use superglue. It is not manufactured for medical use and as such, the manufacturer can change ingredients and formulation without consideration for safety on wounds.

Muzzles are a must. If you need to use your pet first aid kit, it is likely the pet is in pain. Any pet that is in pain is a bite risk.

Plastic baggies to collect a vomit or fecal sample. This may be necessary if the pet has been poisoned and you are unsure of what was ingested. When not in use, it can store smaller items for easy accessibility.

Rubber gloves to protect you from any zoonotic diseases and also to collect vomit or fecal samples.

Sanitary napkins will absorb blood.

Squirt bottle to deliver hydrogen peroxide down the throat of a dog.

Styptic powder for use on nails only. It stings and this pet is already in pain. In addition, styptic powder is not sterile and you may introduce bacteria into the wound.

Black tea bags contain tannic acid. Tea is effective in stopping bleeding.

Vet wrap is wonderful. It keeps the wound secure and

dry. Vet wrap is also expensive. The human counterpart, which is the exact same thing, is a fraction of the cost.

Wound cleanser—You have several options. The first is sterile saline solution, also known as eyewash. The second is a Chlorohexidine based cleanser. This is easy to find. Almost any store that sells first aid items carries it. Do not use hydrogen peroxide as it degrades surrounding tissue and cats cannot metabolize it. Do not use alcohol as it stings. Do not use sterile, tap, or bottled water and it disrupts the salt balance of the cells and slows healing.

Happy Hoodies have many uses, one of which is to keep the pet's ear close to their head in the event of an injury. The hoodie holds the ear in place so that head shaking won't cause further damage to the injured ear.

KY Jelly or vaseline in the event a male dog suffers from paraphimosis. Paraphimosis is a condition in which the penis will not retract back into the sheath.

Many of these items have expiration dates and should be checked periodically. Please note that once a sterile item has been opened it is no longer sterile and needs to be replaced.

Treating injuries quickly result in faster healing with less pain. It may also reduce veterinary costs. Win–win for all.

4

Love Your Business

GOAL:
Learn how to take care of the
health of your business.

"Happiness does not come from doing easy work but from the after-glow of satisfaction that comes after the achievement of a difficult task that demanded our best."

~ Theodore Isaac Rubin

Niche Yourself

Finding your niche can be a lot of fun. Niching is defining a sub-set or segment of a larger group that you want to appeal to. For example, Beth's business's niche is serving dogs 25lbs and under. Some groom cats exclusively, while others may specialize in terriers or non-sporting breeds. You can define your niche as broadly or narrowly as you like, however, take care not to alienate clients you may want to attract.

Sometimes finding your niche is decided for you. As earlier mentioned, Beth only accept pets under 25lbs. This is because after many years of grooming, she developed orthopedic issues with her back. She decided if she wanted to continue grooming, she had to slow down. Beth also realized that it would be better for her staff, reduce the risk of injuries and increase profits. Obviously, it was a no-brainer. She decided to take the plunge and commit to the niche.

When adopting a niche, you need to commit. Change your outgoing voice message to clearly state, *what the niche is.* You may have to refer current clients that no longer met the criteria to other local groomers. This is tough but it makes room for growth. It's one more reason why it is important to have good working relationships with other local groomers. However, you can keep "special" pets that no longer meet your criteria.

Having a specialty helps to focus your marketing efforts. It can set you apart from your competition by creating a unique selling point or "USP." A USP is critical to creating targeted advertising campaigns. Being the local geriatric grooming specialist makes you the authority on the topic. You can use blogs or social media to promote your specialty. Being recognized as the premier anything allows you to charge more for your services.

Keep in mind you should play to your strengths. It is not recommended to cater solely to small dogs if you cannot imagine grooming without Golden Retrievers. It would also not be advised to focus on a breed or group that do not display your talents well. Conversely, just because you love Bichons does not mean you HAVE to be the "Bubbly Bichon Barber." Your business may fare better if you generalize that talent to curly coat types.

Much of the above information may sound contradictory. Rest assured, it is not. It's just another example of how many ways there are to successfully run a mobile grooming business.

A concern that you may have is whether or not there is enough business for a niche groomer to make a living. In Danbury, Connecticut, there are over 9,000 licensed dogs. Add in three surrounding towns and that number jumps to 30,000 licensed dogs. (I make a point of using the word "licensed," as not everyone feels the need to license their pet.) According to the American Veterinary

Medical Association, there are almost an equal number of cats. In a small four-town area, there are upwards of 60,000 pets. The average mobile groomer needs between 150 and 200. To reach that particular group involves targeted marketing, which is covered in another chapter.

Niching may not appeal to you and that's okay too. The important point is to have fun and love what you do!

Love Your Vehicle

Our vehicles are our livelihood. Without them we cannot pay our bills or earn a living. Regular maintenance is the key to keeping your unit in optimal working condition. Maintenance is not just reserved for the engine and is not solely the domain of your mechanic.

It is your responsibility to understand the meaning of all dashboard light indicators. That is why the owner's manual should always remain in the unit, preferably in the protection of the glove box. The lights notify you should the vehicle need attention. The most common lights are fluid related. Most fluids can be easily filled by the operator, however, if you are uncomfortable with that then be sure to have designated maintenance personnel.

Cleaning also falls under the heading of maintenance. This includes inside the cab and grooming area, as well as the exterior of the unit. Seat covers will extend the life of your seats and keep them free from inevitable lunch and coffee spills. Regular washing as well as annual waxing at minimum will keep your unit looking its best and protect against damaging UV rays, salt, and road dirt. A dirty truck, whether inside or out, does not convey the professional image you want to portray. It also does not provide for efficient, happy, or healthy working conditions.

Interior cleaning and maintenance should be performed at regular intervals; after each household, end of the day, end of the week, monthly, quarterly, and annually. When you stay on top of cleaning, it becomes second nature and exponentially easier to manage. We have a suggested cleaning checklist at **www.PawsitiveEd. com/mobile-groomers-bible-resources.** Some grooming matters require regular attention, such as replacing dryer and vacuum brushes, checking battery water levels, and inventorying supplies. These tasks can easily be accomplished with the implementation of checklists and scheduled reminders.

Always keep in mind the resale of your unit. Even if you plan to keep it until you kill it, you never know what life will bring and you may change your mind. If you keep the endgame in sight, you can make better decisions. A clean, well-maintained vehicle will command a higher price.

Love Yourself

"You yourself, as much as anybody in the entire universe, deserve your love and affection" ~ Buddha

Without yourself you have no one. If you do not take care of yourself how can you take care of your business? Self-care is so very difficult for many of us. We are service providers by definition, but we can only take care of others once we have cared for ourselves. That is why we are told to put our oxygen mask on by airline personnel BEFORE helping others.

This industry can be very rewarding IF we take good care of ourselves. We must stay ever vigilant of burn-out. Burn-out is extremely common in this industry. Many are over-worked and underpaid. There is no one to blame for these conditions but the business owner. It is their responsibility to ensure all are compensated fairly, and to provide a safe, functional work environment.

State-of-the-art equipment looks good and has the deeper values of being cost-effective and ergonomically correct. Poorly-maintained equipment affects safety, efficiency, and morale. DIY conversions and equipment can compromise overall performance, which can cost thousands more in repairs and medical bills in the long run. Whenever possible, purchase the best you can afford, it pays dividends.

There is power in the little word "no." There have been volumes written about how to say no. Why is such a tiny, two-letter word so difficult for so many? Possibly because we are afraid using it will in some way disappoint others. That could not be further from the truth. Every time the word "no" is discriminately used, we are actually saying "YES" to a number of other things.

Setting boundaries and having a comprehensive operations manual will provide some frame work as to when saying no is appropriate. For example, if you have operation hours of 9-5 you should be able to comfortably complete 5 to 6 one-hour grooms per day. If a client calls to schedule her two enormous Doodles on a day that already has four 1-hour grooms scheduled, you know the answer is "no." That does not mean you have to use the two-lettered word; you can tell the client, "unfortunately, that day won't work, but we can groom them on..." You have just said "yes" to coming home at a reasonable hour to cook a healthy dinner and have quality time instead of cramming more work into an already full day, possibly even traveling home after dark, increasing the possibility of an accident, all so that you can hit a fast-food joint for dinner and miss out on the kids' bathtime. Catch our drift?

Simple ways to love yourself can be manicures, pedicures, massages, or other personal care products. A good chiropractor is worth their weight in gold. Let's not forget the value of yoga, meditation, and stretching exercises peppered throughout your day. These items are not a frivolous waste of money, but an investment in your most valuable resource, you! Declaring and sticking to regular, posted hours of operation will keep burn out at bay.

For your well-being you should schedule regular days off and vacation. Yes, vacation. This includes providing eligible employees with at least one week's worth of paid time off.

"I don't think of vacation as optional. If I don't have scheduled time to unplug, I am useless to myself, my family, friends, business, staff and clients. That is why I will not regularly schedule weekends and close the first 2 weeks of January annually." ~ Beth

Finally, benefits should not be just for employees. Medical, dental, and disability insurances are necessary. It's not a matter of *if* you'll need them but *when* you'll need them. An unexpected accident or medical emergency can quickly bankrupt anyone. Contact your insurance agent or financial planner for help with acquiring these vital coverages.

Love Your Business

It should be a pleasure to go to work every day. If you are happy, the pets in your care will pick up on your good vibes and be more likely to cooperate. How do you make that pleasure last your career? It is much easier to achieve than you think.

Not to beat a dead horse, but take a vacation. Put it in your planner from the day you start, even if you are not going anywhere. Shut off the computer and phone. Give your brain a chance to reset. You will make better business decisions and allow room for inspiration if you do.

Don't overbook yourself. This is even more important around the holidays. The money could be good, but it comes at the great expense of your physical and mental well-being. Instead, remember to charge appropriately for your services and encourage a regular schedule.

Let go of clients that are not a good fit. Not every client is your client and that's OK. This goes for either the pet or the person. If you dread going to a particular call, LET THEM GO. They will be better served by someone that wants their business. Remember the 30,000 licensed dogs in the greater Danbury area? You would still have over 29,998 dogs to choose from, way more than is needed.

Music should be soothing and relaxing for both groomer and pet. Loud, high-or-low-pitched tones, such as those associated with rap or hard rock, may agitate the pets in your care. Agitated pets are harder to groom.

Agitated pets take longer to groom. Agitated pets are a bite risk. Easy listening, classical, jazz, pop, and talk radio are good choices. Check out the resources for our recommendations.

Crystals have a measure-able energy, measured in hertz. We, too have a measure-able energy measured in hertz. For example, the human brain is a few Hz to 20 Hz, heart beat is 2 Hz, skin is 1000Hz, and eyes are 60 Hz. Energy from crystals and people can affect each other. However, crystals operate at a dominant frequency, meaning it doesn't change much, whereas people's energetics change frequently due to illness, stress, diet, environment, and so forth. Crystals, being stable, can raise our energetic levels by being in proximity to us. So put a piece of rose quartz in your van, tub, and shelf.

Plants naturally clean the air. With care, you can have live plants in a mobile grooming unit. They need sunlight, so should be situated near a window when stationary, but placed in the tub with towels surrounding them when in transit. Air plants are a great choice because they do not require a pot or soil. Many can be easily rooted to grates or wood frames and only require infrequent watering.

Burnout is a real thing for groomers. But it doesn't have to be for you. Simple changes can go a long way.

Storing and Winterizing Your Vehicle

Even if you live in a more tropical area, familiarize yourself with how to store/winterize your vehicle, so you can still work when needed. Know what temperature is unsafe to work in for you and the pets you groom. Wind chill will heavily factor into this equation. The further north you are, the lower this unsafe temperature becomes. In addition to hypothermia or frost bite risks to both groomer and pet, extreme cold temperature can cause vehicle damage if you hit a pothole. While garaging a vehicle is always the best option, it's not always feasible.

Drain gray water as soon as you get home and fill up fresh water at the same time. Full tanks take much longer to freeze than partially filled tanks. If you do not have an inside fresh water fill, try to install one. Use heat tape around waterlines, as well as insulated thermal sheets or blankets. Home improvement stores will have a selection to choose from. Inside the vehicle, take off nozzles and drain as much water from the lines as possible. Thermal pipe wrap and blankets, as well as electric wrap, can be sourced at most hardware stores. In single-digit temperatures, remove the water pump and place it in tub to prevent ice buildup inside the pump. Use ceramic or oil-filled space heaters aimed at plumbing inside the van. In colder temperatures, you may need two.

If the vehicle is going to be parked for more than a couple of days, drain all the water out of all the lines. If you have a stand-alone water heater, drain that as well, but remember to run water through it before turning it back on or you will burn out the heating element. If you have an inverter system, remember to turn it off. It will drain down the batteries after a while if the van is unplugged.

Even though we do everything to prevent water lines from freezing, it still happens. Many times, the pipes and pumps just need a little time to defrost. In such cases, bringing gallons of water from home will get you through the first pet or two without having to reschedule.

If you have a winterizing feature on your conversion, follow their instructions. If you intend to leave a unit unused for an extended period of time (two weeks or more) it is recommended to start the unit at least once a week and let it run for at least an hour. During this time, it is also recommended to use the appliances as they need regular usage too. When equipment is left idle, it tends to break. Regular use keeps things moving and working.

5

Listen to Your Business

GOAL:
Pay attention to the needs and
wants of your clients.

"A satisfied customer is the best business strategy of all."

~ Michael LeBoeuf

What Do Your Clients Want?

Client Surveys

How do you really know what clients want? Better yet, how do you know what your best clients find important? Ask them! A survey is one of the most underrated, yet powerful tools in a marketing toolkit.

What Does A Survey Accomplish?

Improves service by offering actionable insights—Your clients are removing the guesswork by telling you exactly what they do and do not like. It identifies your weaknesses so that you can implement the necessary improvements.

Measures customer satisfaction—You are able to recognize and capitalize on what makes you special, as well as identify your client advocates. Advocates are those wonderful people that you can get testimonials from.

Increases customer retention—You are validating your client's importance to your business. Your business is telling them that their feelings are valued. Clients who feel important are more likely to stay and tell their friends how awesome you are.

New ideas for products and services—Be on the forefront of new marketing trends by offering what other facilities are not.

Sample 5-Question Survey:

"I keep my survey short and to the point. I prefer brief, easy answers as opposed to a number ranking. Number rankings do not give the entire story or offer the insight needed to affect real changes. However, written answers may not be filled out without some sort of hold (return of their pet) or small token (inexpensive gift or coupon)." ~ Mary

1. **What do you like best about my service?** By starting out with a positive, it begins on a constructive, rather than a destructive note. Repeated responses and phrases, such as "reliable" or "trustworthy" can be used for marketing materials such as websites, ads, and brochures. If it is important to current clients, it will attract future customers. It also identifies those clients that are open to a testimonial.

2. **What do you like least about my service?** This identifies areas in need of improvement, particularly if several people mention the same thing. Most of the time it is very specific to the client. They didn't like the shampoo scent or wanted the rear feathering removed or wondered if there are

weekend appointments. All very easily remedied, resulting in very happy clients.

3. **What service would you like to see offered?** This will identify upcoming marketing trends. Even if it is only a handful of people who request a new service, word gets around.

4. **What products would you like to see offered?** Retailing is very possible in a mobile unit. Check out the section detailing how to add retail.

5. **Any thoughts on how I can improve?** This is rather open-ended, and a much harder question to answer. While not always filled out, it can offer incredible insight.

It is as easy to hand the survey to the client upon arrival. If the owner will not be home, email the survey along with their appointment and tell them you will pick it up when you arrive. A 100% fill out rate is possible.

If you have employees, the owner should take charge of this task. If the survey is delivered via employee, they may either forget to distribute the survey or repress the results they feel are a poor reflection of them. Such actions would undermine the goal of the exercise. Instead, you could email the survey to all clients, which may have a low open\return rate. www.SurveyMonkey.com offers both a free and paid version to send surveys by email. Another option is to hand pick a random sample of your clients to call and do a telephone survey.

Surveys can help pinpoint strengths and weaknesses, allowing you to make changes that correspond with the direction you want your business to grow.

Educated Clients Are Good Clients

That bears repeating. Educated clients are good clients. Help them to become good clients. There should not be an assumption that, because you know how to do something, everyone does. There are many ways to go about educating your clients.

In person—Talk it up during the first contact. This is your first impression. Wow them. Go beyond telling them what you do and what it costs. Ask them about their pet and their lifestyle. Make recommendations tailored to their needs. This person has contacted you and wants to know more about your business. Seize the opportunity to teach them. During check-in, do an assessment and make recommendations that will address your findings. Topics could include how to comb and brush the pet, oral care, diet, and so forth. It's a good time to discuss your policies.

Newsletter—As there are federal laws regarding newsletters, it's best to use a service. Mailchimp, while limited, is free. Other services such as Constant Contact, Aweber, Active Campaign, ConvertKit, and Drip are fee based. Do your research and find a service that will keep you compliant with laws as well as serve your needs. A newsletter could include some tips, articles and blogs of interest, any specials or new services, highlight a client's pet, and so forth. A newsletter, even if not opened, brings your business to mind when they see it in their inbox.

Facebook business page—According to Facebook's Terms of Services, you must use a business page to promote your business. It's free in the sense that you don't pay for the page, but you can most certainly pay for ads. Paid Facebook ads can be tricky to be cost effective. Here is where paying for an expert will save you money in the long run. Your business page can be used to interact with your existing clients as well as potential clients. Resist the urge to engage in "Like Ladders" with your business page. A Like Ladder is when you swap "Likes" with other groomers (not your clients) to increase the number of "likes" on your page. DON'T DO IT. Facebook only shows a percentage of your business posts to those that liked it. Would you rather another groomer see that post or a client? Fill out the Facebook business page information in its entirety, especially the address. To see an example of a business page, visit Daryl Conner's at: www.facebook.com/fairwindsgroomingstudio/

Instagram is a picture-based social media platform. To be effective, take a workshop. There is only 24 hours in a day and you want time spent on any platform to have a measurable outcome.

Website—It's a must and will be covered in the marketing section.

Educated clients can make better decisions about the care of their pet. If you provide that education, you will be viewed as the expert and "go-to" for any questions they may have.

Showcase Yourself

"One day I get to a client's house and I can tell she's just bubbling with excitement. She had a story to tell. She was waiting in the school parking lot with another parent and they were trying to outdo each other with who had the better groomer. After the third round, they realized they had the same groomer. ME." ~ Mary

Everybody likes to feel special and that they have made good choices. Clients aren't mind readers, they only know how special you are if you let them know.

Things to share:

- Continuing education. Take pictures at trade shows and post them on social media. Frame the certificates of any courses and display them in your van. Laminate them first.

- Display all awards and trophies.

- Have new products? Tell all individually that you have chosen them to try out a new product and you value their feedback.

- Let the client know what grooming entails with an informative handout.

The more they know about you and how your business operates, the more comfortable they become. At times, what appears to be a demeaning question such as, "You are going to cut their nails, right?" Or "You aren't going to hurt him, are you?", is simply because the client doesn't understand what we do. These questions are an opportunity to educate, rather than become defensive and alienating them.

Marketing

"Build it and they will come" marketing only works in the movies. Add in the fact that people need to see an advertisement 13 times before recognizing it and marketing to the masses becomes less effective as it dilutes the message. The result is a depleted or an overextended marketing budget when trying to reach the general population.

The American Pet Product Association estimates that there are currently 66.75 billion pets in the United States to the tune of seven out of ten pet owning families.

"Danbury, Connecticut, alone boasts over 9,000 licensed dogs. Include a couple of surrounding towns and that number jumps to around 30,000." ~ Mary

There is plenty to go around. The pet industry is a huge market to tap and the bottom line is that most small businesses cannot accommodate that volume. Instead, spend those marketing dollars wisely by targeting your ideal clients.

Identifying Your Ideal Client

What is their demographic? This includes type of pets, number of average pets per household, age, sex, income, and spending habits. The smaller the demographic group, the more focused marketing becomes.

A single mobile pet groomer needs less than 150 regular pets to be successful. Three sites to find demographic information:

a. www.suburbanstats.com,

b. www.avma.org/KB/Resources/Statistics/Pages/ Market-research-statistics-US-pet-ownership. aspx, and,

c. www.americanpetproducts.org.

What do they want? This can be approached in two different ways. The first is to find out what is needed and then provide it. The second is to offer what you are passionate about and convince clients (marketing) they want it. Figure out either or both with a Client/Competitor/Your Business Venn Diagram.

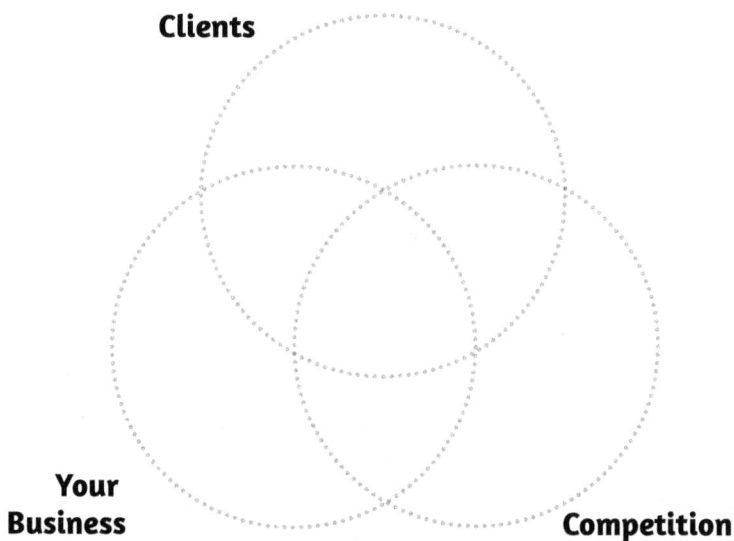

Clients

Your Business

Competition

It's easier to start with competition. What are they doing or selling that is working well for them? What are their/your specialties? Handstripping, elderly pets, puppy's first groom, or hard-to-handle pets are examples. What can you do better or with a twist? This exercise can identify both your similarities and differences to other local businesses. It becomes your choice to design a marketing plan that appeals to what makes you better, or one that highlights your unique perspective. This exercise can also help to identify types of customers that are not your ideal clients.

Now you know who your clients are and what they want. How do you find them?

Tell your friends and family. Practice your elevator speech with them. An "elevator speech" is a term that refers to a brief conversation in which you describe what you do in the amount of time it takes to go from one floor to another in an elevator. It's more than just a statement. It conveys your passion and why a potential client would be interested in your goods or services. A mobile groomer's might be "I groom cats and dogs in a nurturing, respectful spa-like environment in my state-of-the-art mobile grooming van, conveniently and in your driveway." This clearly indicates the benefits of what is offered, as opposed to simply stating you groom dogs in a mobile grooming van.

Target your message in niche and weekly publications. If you're not sure if the publication is a good fit, contact the publisher for audience profiles. If you have never designed an ad, let their design team do it for you. It's worth the investment.

Google—In any given day, there are 3.5 billion searches on Google by people looking for a website to solve their problem. While you can put up a quick and cheap website on your own, it may not be effective if you are unfamiliar with what brings your website to the top of a search. In addition, consider adding a blog to your website. Blogs can extend your reach by offering sought after information that is connected to your website.

Set up a Facebook business page along with other social media sites. Each platform has its own way of reaching potential clients. Research which sites will be to your advantage to spend time on. There are plenty of online programs that can help you navigate through the maze and confusion of using social media effectively. Google "How to use social media for business." Or ask friends for recommendations.

Get out in the real world and meet people. Almost any live event may be a good fit as 70% of all household's own pets. That means that 7 out of 10 people walking past your booth are a potential client. Pet shelters usually have at least one event every year. Join a www.MeetUp.com local pet or business group. While there is a yearly charge if you organize a MeetUp group, it's free to join one that is already set up.

Printed materials such as business cards, brochures, and flyers are needed to hand out at events. Local printing shops can offer an experienced hand in helping you design marketing materials, but services like Vistaprint are cheaper. As a business card may be the first impression of your business, quality should be the first consideration over expense.

Network with local business referral associations such as Alignable and Chambers of Commerce.

Putting the time and effort into identifying who, what, and where your ideal client is can help you focus your marketing dollars into an effective plan.

The cornerstone of any effective marketing plan employs consistency, clarity, and professionalism. Working in tandem, these three principles will help a business's visibility and increase their credibility.

Consistency

Consistency must be across the board. That includes websites, Facebook pages, business cards, brochures, newsletters, emails, and other forms of media. If all your marketing materials are different or you consistently change it up, it makes it harder for potential clients to identify with your business.

In addition, consistency is paramount for online

searches. Google and Yahoo's 'bots will consider differences as independent businesses, resulting in lower search rankings. A "bot" is an automated program that has a specific job. Search bots will look for exact matches, but can't differentiate between slight differences.

If, for example, this is how your business is listed on these sites:

Facebook—http://www.website.com, 123 Main St, 555-4567

Yelp—www.website.com, 123 Main Street, 555-4567

Yahoo—www.website.com, 123 Main Street, (123)-555-4567

Foursquare—http://www.website.com, 123 Main St., and (123)-555-4567

A search engine 'bot, would consider these to be four separate businesses. While it may be time consuming initially, going through all of the listing services to ensure they are exactly the same may elevate your search rankings.

Clarity

Do potential clients know what you do?

Professional marketers agree that you have nine seconds to get your point across before a potential client moves on. Your nine seconds has to be clear on what you offer and what problem you solve for that person. Why should they use your services? What sets you apart from your competition? Will your website and Facebook page hold someone's attention so they will read further?

Your nine seconds could follow this format:

I help_____ (people you help)
Who_____ (problem you solve)
Feel _____.

Mary's nine seconds is:

I help pet owners,
who are looking for a holistic, compassionate approach
*   to grooming,*
feel confident about leaving their beloved pet at the
*   groomers."*

Your nine-second message should be on your Facebook business page, website, brochures, and business cards.

What's wonderful about business cards is that it makes your nine seconds permanent. Magnetic cards are great because they always end up on a refrigerator where a potential client will walk past your message many times a day.

Clarity also means readability. Is your material hard to read? Fonts that are tiny or in script, dark lettering on dark backgrounds, or light lettering on light backgrounds, may be difficult to decipher. Does your marketing material stand out from the pack, or are you using the same design as other pet professionals in your area?

"I recently attended a networking conference where 18 of the 42 business cards I collected were unreadable while 15 had the exact same design." ~ Mary

Professionalism

While you do not need to hire a professional, your marketing materials should look professional. Sites such as www.Picmonkey.com, and www.Canva.com make it easy to design social media headers, logos, and business cards. You may opt to hire a professional when it comes time to design your logo or ads.

Many website hosts offer site-builder tools or access to Wordpress. However, it may be a worthwhile investment to hire a professional as a website doesn't even get nine seconds of consideration from a prospective client.

A study done by Stanford University found that 75% of people made a judgment about a business by its website in .05 seconds. That's half a second. That's the time it takes to look at the portion of your website that appears when someone visits. Add in a report by Fleishman-Hilliard that 89% of people now search online for services, and you realize that the top third of your homepage is the most important part of your website. It will determine whether or not a potential client will keep reading or click away. In addition, the number of mobile users is growing exponentially. Is your website mobile device friendly? Visit your website from your phone and see how it appears.

That half second won't matter if your website does not show up in a search. A professional can help with keywords and listing with search engines. A "keyword" is the word or words a user puts in the search bar when they are looking for a service. These words need to be on your website, preferably in a heading. It should include town, name of business, and pet/dog/cat mobile grooming.

Let's talk about Google a little bit more. They are the king of Internet searches, with an average of 3.5 billion searches every day. Plus, they own the Chrome browser. They have instituted 2 new rules.

First, to "protect" users from fraudulent sites, Google is requiring that all websites have a basic SSL (Secure Sockets Layer) certificate. The purpose of this certificate is to provide an extra layer of security between your computer and any site. It changes "http" to "https." It provides that little green padlock symbol you see on the browser bar of some websites.

Without this certificate, anyone visiting your website will get a warning that this site may be unsafe. That will drastically reduce the number of people going to your site. This rule is already in effect. If you're not sure you really need to bother with this. Head over to the Chrome browser and put your website in the search bar. That is how your site will appear to potential clients.

Have your host provider install this certificate. It should run you anywhere from $10-30 a year. DO NOT USE cheaper third-party software. Have your website provider do a 301 redirect as well. The certificate is meaningless without a 301 redirect. If you don't know what it is, then don't attempt on your own. A 301 redirect is a piece of code added to your website. That's usually another $50 one-time fee.

Even after obtaining the SSL certificate and 301 redirect, you may not see the padlock on the browser bar. To find out why, go to www.whynolock.com and follow the directions. Usually, the problem is an uploaded photo that, once removed, resolves the problem.

The second is only important if you have a pop-up on your site. A pop-up encourages people to sign up for your newsletter. If they consider your pop up intrusive, then they will blacklist your site for mobile applications. Pop-up dimensions can appear much larger on mobile devices. If you are uncertain if your pop-up is annoying Google, visit your website from your phone. If it appears quickly or takes up the screen, then its intrusive and you need to fix that. If you don't know how, contact your pop-up provider.

Google is the search engine of choice by billions of users. Don't reduce the likelihood of potential clients finding your site. These are pretty easy changes to make. If you think this is beyond your capabilities, then let your website hosting company do it for you.

Press Release

A well-written press release is free advertising, with an emphasis on "well-written." If all an editor needs to do is copy and paste, it's more likely to see print. In addition, business editors are always on the lookout for feel-good articles on local businesses. You can't put a dollar amount on the exposure your business will receive from an article.

Elements of a good press release:

- Keep it businesslike.

- Leave out the adjectives and adverbs.

- Just the facts.

This can be adapted if you are just starting out, getting a new van, adding a specialty service, or adding retail. Anything that is different is cause to write and submit press releases. Continuous contact with potential clients will keep you in the front of their mind.

Information on where to send your press release can usually be found on the newspaper's website or on the second or third page of the print newspaper.

An example of a new-hire press release is on the following page:

FOR IMMEDIATE RELEASE NEW HIRE (name of hire)

Created: (Date)

(Name of business) hire (name) as (job title)

(Name of business) is pleased to announce the addition of (name) to the (name of business) team. (name) brings (list skills and qualifications).

(Quote by new hire on why she wants to work there.)

(Any change to services or schedules, or types of animals seen should be mentioned in this paragraph.)

(Last paragraph is on the business and what it brings to the community.)

Live Events

Though there is more to attending a live event than just showing up, proper planning can make your day lively and without incident, as opposed to boring or problematic.

What type of events do you want to participate in?

The list here can be endless: craft fairs, pet adoption days, shelter events, town events, etc. It really doesn't matter what event you go to because a survey by the American Pet Products Association found that nearly 65% of families own a pet. That means at least six out ten people that walk past your table owns a pet.

Your local newspaper should have a listing of all upcoming events. If you belong to a chamber of commerce, you will most likely receive an email invitation to buy booth space at upcoming events.

How much should you spend on a booth?

Consider your ROI or Return on Investment. Prices range from free to a couple thousand dollars. Will you generate the clients to cover the cost of the booth? Some events will trade booth space in exchange for providing a free service such as nail trimmings, or a short informational talk.

What do you need to consider when choosing a venue?

Are they providing table and chairs? If not, you will need to provide them. If you plan on attending several events, the investment in a table and chair will be around $100 new.

Will you need electricity or Wi-Fi? Sometimes a venue includes these services for free or for a nominal fee if the service is available.

If indoor or sheltered booth space is not available, you will need a tent. Do one event under the sun and as soon as you get home, you will order a pop-up tent for the next event. Cheaper is not better when it comes to these tents. Expect to pay about $130 for a new one. The inexpensive ones are hard to put up and take down, and the first good breeze will send them sailing.

For mobile groomers, will they allow you to bring your van or trailer to act as your booth?

What Should You Bring to Events?

Bottled water for you, as well as a water bowl for dogs passing by.

A bowl of candy for people and one for pet treats to entice people stopping by your table. As a general rule, people will stop and open the candy, giving you an opportunity to pitch your services. Sometimes there are food vendors at events, but usually there is a long line.

Promotional material such as business cards, brochures, or coupons. Consider a treat bag with a business card attached. Loose business cards have a way of getting lost at the bottom of bags and forgotten. Magnetic cards are better as they usually end up on a refrigerator.

Raffle off an inexpensive gift bag. Make sure it is pet specific. You only want pet owners putting their names and emails into the jar. Once you have their emails, you have a way to contact potential clients through a newsletter.

Gift bags are offered by many events coordinators to all participants. Make sure they have something of yours to add to the bag. It can be a coupon or an inexpensive item that has your business information on it such as a personalized lead.

Raffle items, such as a gift certificates are collected by many events, with proceeds going to a local shelter or rescue.

Bring a friend so you can hit the potty or visit the other booths.

Your booth should be attractively laid out and inviting with a nice table covering. Call attention to yourself. Vistaprint has a large, inexpensive selection of banners and event posters.

TALK TO PEOPLE ABOUT YOUR SERVICES. Make an impression.

How to Market an Event

- Create flyers to hand out to your clients.

- Send out a newsletter detailing the event.

- Post the event on your Facebook business page.

- Livestream the event from your Facebook business page, and save it for future marketing.

Live events give you the opportunity for potential clients to see the passion you have for your business shine through, as well as educate them why you are the pet groomer for them.

Retail

If only five clients purchased $20 a week from you, that adds almost an extra $5,000 a year. Now imagine if 20 clients purchased $20 a week in retail; that will add $20,000 to your bottom line. You can make it easy for them to purchase from you, rather than getting in their car and driving to the store. So much easier to have it delivered at time of grooming or even dropped shipped directly.

Drop Shipping is done one of two ways. There are services such as www.PetDropShipper.com (a full-service online pet store where you set up a webpage on their site. Your clients will order directly from that site, and it is shipped directly to them, and you get a check from the site. The other way is through affiliate links on someone else's website. The company in question will give you a specific link for your clients to order from. They track those orders and send you a check. Phillips Pet is trying out something similar and may be offering the same service as well.

Design and print out a catalog. Leave it at your client's house and let them place an order before the next appointment. Or send a digital copy of your catalog when you send them a text or email reminder of their next day's appointment. This requires stock on hand.

Another option is a printed catalog. However, it is not always on your client's kitchen counter. You will have to consistently remind them you offer this service.

Impulse items such as cookies, toys, collars, leashes, and dental products do not take up much room and can be kept in a sampler box in your vehicle.

If you are not sure what products to start with, consider a trip to Superzoo in Vegas. It is the largest pet retail trade show in the U.S. with miles and miles of vendor booths. Retail is very doable with minimal space and a little creativity.

6

Imagine Where Your Business Can Take You

GOAL:
Recognize and plan for growth.

"Ideas pull the trigger, but instinct loads the gun."

~ Don Marquis

Document Your Process

What is a system? According to Merriam-Webster, a system is "an organized set of doctrines, ideas, or principles usually intended to explain the arrangement or working of a systematic whole." Simply put, it is an organized way of doing something. We use systems in all aspects of life.

Many of us use systems to get through our morning preparations. Wake up, make coffee, use bathroom, start breakfast, and so forth. They are an integral way of getting through the day while maintaining order. They help us run on autopilot, allowing us to do things while not really thinking about them. Remember back to that first dog you groomed to breed specification. How long did it take? Did you have a small anxiety attack about the viability of making a living wage? You knew there was a better way. That's the beauty of systems.

Often, if the system is not adhered to, chaos prevails. Things get lost, forgotten or at the very least, time is wasted. An extreme example is, while driving, all vehicle operators are supposed to adhere to the right-of-way system. It is designed to ensure a safe experience for all motorists and their passengers. However, if it is not observed, confusion, anxiety and dangerous conditions can result.

Why systematize your business? Systems can increase efficiency, speed, productivity, and your business's financial health, giving you more time to enjoy life as you see fit. Most companies that run like "well-oiled machines" often employ the use of systems.

We see that, when we reduce most daily activities to a systematized science, we optimize our efforts. Everyone knows what to expect, including the pets. Nothing is forgotten and as the pets become accustomed to this routine, our work goes faster and we are more efficient. But, it's imperative to structure your business around systems as well. They help lay the foundation for your enterprise. EVERYTHING can be systematized! Even the way you answer the phone. The process is not meant to dull-out or cookie-cutter your business's processes, but to facilitate an efficient execution.

You can make your systems as simple, elaborate, funky, or fun as you like. The point is to make sure things get done the same way every time. Clients like a dependable outcome. What they may like most about a business is that it is reliable. Reliability does not happen by accident. It is a direct result of following a system or group of systems.

Now that you understand the concept and function of systems let's talk about how to create systems. Believe it or not, you already have many systems at work. Now the key is to document those systems. The way a dog is washed, the way you clean your tools, the way you complete paperwork. Eventually, every process should be systematized and documented.

Once documented they can be passed onto staff to tangibly show how you want the job done. When introducing your systems to others it is important to be prepared to explain why you want things done the way you have prescribed. This can be an excellent learning opportunity for all. Systems can always be improved. New products, tools and techniques may be introduced to the market that makes sense for your business. Embrace them and adjust your systems accordingly.

In addition to documenting your business practices, adding a morning journaling routine can increase your focus on what is necessary to run your business. A journal details your expectations for the day. What needs to be accomplished? By writing it in a journal, a connection is made in your brain to get it done.

"I journal every morning. Everything gets done, sometimes to my surprise." ~ Mary

Organizational Chart

Organizational charts or "org charts" are a great way to view all tasks and positions within your operation at-a-glance. Not everyone in your organizational chart will be an employee. Some positions may be held by independent contractors such as accountants or lawyers. Still other duties may be filled by businesses whose services you purchase, such as a sharpener or mechanic. It is vital to classify workers appropriately. Incorrect classification is a crime, which can carry hefty fines and unnecessary aggravation.

Org charts identify where you may have staffing needs. Conversely, they may uncover where you need to redistribute responsibilities or make cuts. These distinctions will be more important than ever with the rising cost of minimum wage, a growing trend across the nation.

"My county's minimum wage is scheduled to increase by $6.00 over the next 5 years!" ~ Beth.

This means more duties should be delegated to some positions.

It can be a fun exercise to create your org chart. Make a pot of your favorite tea and brainstorm a list of every duty performed in your business. I mean every tiny function. No matter how small or insignificant it may seem, write it down. Once you have compiled that list, group related tasks together. Assign a department classification to each group such as operations, finance etc. Then arrange the list of duties into job titles.

The title and subsequent duties will lay the foundation for the job description. Descriptions are essential. They clearly define who is responsible for what tasks and what pre-requisites are essential to the position. Knowing this information ahead of time streamlines the interview process, increasing efficiency and maintaining compliance with the law. It can guide you through the composition of effective help-wanted ads.

Org charts and job descriptions should delineate the chain-of-command. It is imperative to know who reports to whom in each situation. A formal chain-of-command eliminates overstepping boundaries and allows staff and contractors to complete their jobs with the peace of mind that someone has "their back."

While a business owner certainly wears many hats, he or she should not bear the burden of every job. If you feel overwhelmed by the amount of responsibility on your plate, a well-thought-out organizational chart can show you where and what to delegate. Think about what you want to do and do what you do best, focus your efforts on those tasks and hire someone to do the rest.

Employees Yes Or No?

So, you think you want employees. Are you sure? Of course not! The idea of becoming an employer can conjure up nightmarish monsters or dreamlike fantasies. I assure you neither extreme is reality.

First, you must decide if you need or want them. If you have a need for staff but you don't want an employee, the decision is made and proceed no further. Listen to your gut don't second guess yourself. On the other hand, don't get confused by your reactions. If you see a need for an employee and are afraid or scared of the unknown, that is natural and healthy. Proceed with caution and soak up all the knowledge you can get your hands on. Journaling about thoughts and feelings can put things into perspective and help you arrive at solid conclusions.

Take the time to figure out why you do or don't want staff. Some find the idea of leaving a legacy appealing.

"For me, I was just plain tired. I had been grooming full-time for more than 15 years. It was beginning to take a toll on my body. I was washing my disabled dog one afternoon and, as my back was screaming, I had an epiphany. I knew it was time to hire staff or sell the business. I could no longer push-through every day." ~ Beth

Your "why" may evolve or change over time. You may find new reasons to support or contradict your decisions. Having a clear understanding of why you chose what you chose is important. There will be many road-blocks on this journey and a clear "why" can help you through the detours.

Becoming an employer is a deeply personal decision. Of course, it is always a good idea to poll opinions, but you must consider that others are not you. You have taken the time to carefully build your business. You've had control over every detail. Are you ready to lose some of that control? Is it time to pass off a few of the hats you wear to another?

You will need to decide what job (description) you want to fill. You may not truly need a stylist at this point. Perhaps a receptionist would suffice to handle office work and administrative duties. That could free you up to groom more pets, if desired. Look at your company's org chart and see which tasks can be rearranged into a new job if you do not want another groomer at this time. A paid intern might be the answer at this point. This is the perfect solution for a business not quite ready to support an experienced groomer. It is a successful model for cultivating the company culture and maintaining the product quality you want while growing your clientele.

Help Wanted!

Once you know you need staff, the next hurdle to jump is finding that special someone. Consult your org chart to figure out what position you need to fill. Use the job description to appeal to potential applicants. Allow the job description to guide your search to optimize your efforts. There's no point in interviewing someone that does not meet the basic criteria you have set forth in the job description.

Everyone wants to know where to find good employees. The answer is, look everywhere… friends, family, clients and of course, online. Be open about what you are trying to accomplish and share with others. You may be surprised what can happen.

"One of my employees was formerly a client's housekeeper, another was referred by my mother's hairdresser."
~ Beth

If you are searching online be sure to target the right market. Grooming social sites and Facebook groups are a targeted place to start.

Once you have decided where to advertise, you will have to design your ad. There is nothing worse than stating just the bare facts and nothing else. For example:

Wanted full-time experienced groomer for busy salon, must be available weekends, cats are a plus. Call…

That ad is neither inspirational nor motivational in any way. It does little to inform the applicant about the company and appears as though little effort was expended. You will only get out what you put in. If that is like the ad you post, prepare for little response. If you do get a response it is unlikely to be from your dream staffer.

Design your ad to get attention and excite the reader. It is more about the company than the applicant. You should sell your company from the start and stand out from competitors, just as you would when marketing to clients. This is marketing to employees. Wherever possible, include an image. Pictures get attention. The contents of the job description should be sprinkled throughout the ad. A better ad would be:

Love to groom? We do too! Pretty Paws LLC is a busy mobile grooming business looking for a conscientious pet stylist. Flexible days/hours are available, no weekends necessary. Our clients are 25lbs and under. Schedule a "ride-along," and see our state-of-the-art units in action. Applicant must be able to complete five small grooms per 8-hour day and have a valid driver's license. Strong customer care skills are necessary. Generous compensation plus tips. This is a wonderful opportunity for a motivated individual who enjoys working in a low-stress environment. Come join our family of valued pet professionals!

Have fun creating help-wanted advertisements. The goal is to attract quality talent that will thrive in your environment. Make that vision clear in your designs and be sure to convey the culture of your business. The more energy you devote to this process the better candidates you will have.

Applicants and the Hiring Process

Let's face it, the hiring process can be nerve racking. Obsessing over the "right" person for the job can lead to sleepless nights. Rest assured, just like everything else we learn there will be mistakes. You will likely kiss a lot of toads until you find the right fit. Just as you took the time to write an irresistible employment ad, take your time with the selection process. You probably would not run to the altar with your first crush. Why hire the first job applicant?

Do not rush into an employment arrangement. It is expensive to train new staff. You want to make the best selections prior to investing your time, money, and energy into a new addition. Don't allow yourself to be governed by fear. Thoughts like, "I need help NOW, I can't turn away clients" or "What if no one else applies?" are nothing more than scare tactics. Don't be afraid of the boogeyman. If an applicant does not meet your criteria, or if you don't have a good feeling about them, then move on. There will be another opportunity.

"I recommend designing a rigorous application process. Doing so will sift the diamonds from the rough" ~ Beth

Going against your inner-voice can have devastating effects. The new hire could cause personnel malcontent, which can rot a business's character and make the workplace an unhappy place. Listen to your intuition and let it be your guide. A lengthy, multi-faceted hiring process gives both the applicant and the company an opportunity to see if they will be a good fit.

When applicants reach out, be ready to welcome them and have your application process ready to go. Once you have applicants, you have a legal obligation to be fair! Write out your application process, then follow it for EVERY applicant to avoid a discrimination claim.

First impressions are important. Upon contacting your company, did the applicant follow any instructions set forth in your employment ad? Did they include a resume, portfolio, or references? If so, verify them before reaching out to the applicant. You may be able to glean useful decision-making information from those resources.

Keep notes of everything, but beware that any written notes made during the interview process are "on the record," so be mindful of what you write. ALL paperwork related to an employee should go in their own file which is required to be locked and private. It is an employee's right to view their file upon request. Therefore, any information contained in their file should be factual documentation related to performance, progress and legal forms.

Even if you decide not to hire an applicant, keep their paperwork. We all change, mature, and grow. They may be a good fit down the road and it's good to have solid intelligence to reflect upon.

After initial contact, set up a telephone interview

with the candidate. Keep the conversation brief and on topic. There are many subjects that are illegal to inquire about such as, age, national origin, color, religion, gender identity, sexual orientation, pregnancy status, disability, or genetic information. Avoid any questions related to such topics. If an applicant begins to divulge protected information, steer the conversation back to work-related topics. If the phone interview goes well, schedule an in-person interview.

The face-to-face interview should take place with the mobile unit available. For example, you can schedule the interview to take place at your local coffee house but park the unit in the lot so the applicant can view their potential workspace. Their reactions can be very telling. It is only fair for them to get a chance to know you and your business too.

Have an application packet prepared for the first in-person interview. Common contents of the application packet are: employment application, questionnaire, and job description. For the sake of professionalism and organization, all paperwork should be printed and presented to the applicant in a folder. The application and questionnaire should be briefly reviewed to clarify any questions then put to the side for later digestion. The job description is for the applicant to keep.

Be open and appear friendly. Listen closely to what the applicant has to say. Observe if they arrive in a timely manner. Pay attention to how they present themselves. Are they clean and tidy? Do they appear confident? Have a few standard questions to help break the ice. It is fair to ask them to tell you about themselves. Ask open-ended questions, allowing them to provide you with their thoughts and philosophies. Show them the unit and if all parties are still interested, schedule the ride-along with demo groom(s). Be sure to mention the demo day is pending background check results.

References are a vital part of the hiring process. Ask for personal and professional references. Even if you learn nothing new about the applicant from the reference check, you learn about the people the applicant surrounds themselves with. Many collect references but fail to follow up on them. This is a foolish practice that can potentially waste your resources. You pay a premium for insurance to protect your business, you should protect that investment with secure practices. Take the time to check references. There stands much to be lost if you hire the wrong person. Leave no stone unturned.

Following the reference checks, it is wise to do employment driver's license, credit checks, and drug testing. You must obtain the applicant's written permission to run these reports. If they do not give their permission, it is within your federal rights to reject the application with cause. A credit check will inform you as to how they relate to financial matters. Obviously, you want to know their criminal and driving history since they will be representing your business, using your equipment, in your client's homes, and handling company finances.

These inquiries include personal information you need to know.

Your insurance agent will run their driving record when adding a new employee to your staff. They may not be able to offer exact findings but they can counsel you about whether their record is of concern.

The duration of the demo ride along should be at least two households. An entire day is preferable. This gives the applicant the opportunity to see the entire process, including traveling between calls. While at the first house, briefly explain the equipment so they can operate at the next appointment. Try not to be critical if they have difficulty adjusting to your facility. Understand this person is in a completely foreign environment and under pressure to perform well.

After demo day find a way to "thank" the individual for their time. I recommend a gift certificate for two to a local restaurant. If you have found your prince or princess, then extend an employment proposal on a trial basis for three months. Either party has the right to walk away at any time during that period with no hard feelings. Still unsure? Schedule another ride-along or tell them you will reach out within a week with your decision.

The authors of this book are NOT labor lawyers. Therefore, you need to consult with state and local (where applicable) departments of labor for counsel. They can be a valuable resource of information for most things employee related. Attend workshops and utilize the mentoring programs offered by these offices. Claiming ignorance of the law is not an acceptable plea in court.

Legal Requirements

The following section is a brief overview of employer requirements. It is by no means a complete resource or replacement for sound legal advice. There are basic federal obligations for all employers. Some states and local municipalities have more specific requirements. Therefore, it is best to consult with your local labor department and/or lawyer for applicable specifications.

A workman's compensation policy is required by law for ALL employees. This is not optional coverage. This coverage is there to protect your staff should they be injured on the job. Unfortunately, many workers are mis-classified in our industry, leaving the business vulnerable to legal action and the employee unprotected should disaster strike. Please read the "worker classification" section for more information.

OSHA requires a "Material Safety Data Sheet" for EVERY product used in your operation. These sheets should be included in the handbook. Go to OSHA's website to determine what is required for your business. There are different requirements depending on a company's size.

Payroll taxes must be collected and submitted for all wages paid. It is recommended to hire a payroll company to do payroll. It's money well spent, doing an important task most are not comfortable processing. Additionally, most large payroll firms have benefits such as medical and retirement planning available for their clients.

New Hire Orientation

Now that you have hired Mr. or Mrs. "Perfect" it is time to get them "drinking your Kool-aid." They have already had the opportunity to observe how you run your operation, now they must be shown how the magic is created.

Every new hire must be presented with the new hire packet. This packet will contain an array of forms. Federal law requires you to keep updated W-4, tax form and I-9, employment eligibility verification form. We recommend additionally retaining a signed handbook acknowledgement, non-compete agreement, and any other documents your state labor department requires. Once completed, all forms are to be stored in the employee's personnel file.

You are urged to consult with your attorney when drawing up a non-compete agreement. They are difficult to enforce and must be specifically worded to allow someone the opportunity to be gainfully employed upon leaving your company.

When a new member joins the team, the manager should verify all support materials such as laminated checklists, pricing information and handbooks are available and in good condition. Often, they need to be replaced or refreshed.

All new staffers should be paired with an adept, proficient employee for at least the first six weeks of employment. Yes, that is two groomers working together during the first six weeks. This length of time allows for in-depth training of using company facilities and evaluation of the new employee's skills. The end of six-week probation should culminate with an evaluation. The evaluation should reflect the entire 6 weeks and determines whether they continue with the company and if they can fly solo or require more training under a senior employee.

Initial probation is a critical time for new hires. It is during this time that they form lasting opinions and habits. As the business owner, you want their experiences to be positive and fruitful. You want to empower them with all the tools needed to be successful. When they are successful, your company is successful too! Ensure only exemplary employees have the honor of orienting new hires. Their positivity and good work habits will encourage the newbie to optimally perform.

Conversely, if you allow a new hire to wade through orientation without effective guidance, they will most likely be uninspired and be forced to make many assumptions (interpretations) about how your operation functions. This can be detrimental to an entity's goals, and a plan to fail for both the employee and the company. If you fail to plan, you plan to fail.

Topics to Be Covered During Probation/Orientation

Driving—If the employee will be expected to drive the unit, it is recommended to give them ample opportunity to adjust to the nuances of driving a larger vehicle. Never force someone to drive if they are not ready. It will only create unnecessary anxiety and unsafe conditions. At first, driving lessons should be short and quick, leading to more time behind the wheel as they gain confidence. Once parking lot exercises have been mastered, move onto the open road. Local roads first and highway driving last. Some folks never get the hang of maneuvering a large vehicle. That is fine, however, they may not be a good fit for your company. Perhaps they can work as an assistant or solely on multiple pet household days scheduled for 2 groomers.

Familiarization of supplies, equipment, and maintenance. Each grooming unit is different. Even if the new hire has previous mobile experience, they should be given a tour that explains the function of all equipment and its maintenance requirements.

Technical grooming skills of the newbie should be observed and evaluated throughout orientation. Notes should be collected to allow for an in-depth evaluation of the employee's performance during the first six weeks. Note areas that exceed, meet, and do not meet company standards. Any criticism should be constructive and delivered in an empowering manner.

Housekeeping—Cleaning, handbook comprehension and paperwork completion. Remember, there are many ways to arrive at a conclusion. As long as company policies and procedures are being adhered to, employees should be encouraged to find the best solution for their needs. During this introductory period, ensure managerial staff remain readily available for any questions that may arise.

Client relations—Ensure your staff understands how to interact with your clients. Role playing exercises may help to find weaknesses, while boosting the confidence of your staff.

Handbooks

For simple purposes the company handbook is a compilation of all operations related documents typically stored in a binder.

- Policies

- Procedures

- Checklists

- Forms

- Organizational chart(s)

- Job descriptions

This is your company's BIBLE. EVERY staff member is to be furnished with a handbook. If you have taken the time to document your systems, compiling a handbook shouldn't be an intimidating task. A copy of all forms, OSHA MSDS sheets, and job descriptions should be included in your handbook/Policy & Procedure manual. Any resource an employee may require should be stored in this binder. The handbook should always be available in all workplaces.

The last page should be a form every employee signs stating they have read, understand and will abide by the handbook while representing your business. EVERY amendment/update must be accompanied by the same sign-able form. When distributing updates be sure to refresh the shop copies too!

Providing a strong P&P manual or handbook is even more important for a mobile operation. It will speak on your behalf and empowers your staff to make well-informed decisions that are in line with your company's culture.

Many folks think the words "policy" and "procedure" are interchangeable. In fact, they are not. They are different words encompassing two similar but different concepts. Policies clearly outline your company's principles, rules, boundaries, and expectations. Procedures explain how the policy is to be carried out, ideally with step-by-step instructions. Policies also detail how to carry out job-related tasks. A policy is what you want; the procedure is how to achieve what you want.

Policy example:
Maintaining high standards of salon cleanliness requires every employee to do their part. A pleasant, hygienic work environment characteristic of professionals promotes morale and contributes to the success the business.

Procedure example:
Use cleaning solutions according to instructions. Always return cleaning solutions to their storage locations when finished. Do not place cleaning supplies around pets; they might be confused with grooming supplies resulting in an injury.

Disinfect counter/table tops and tools after every pet with the appropriate cleaning supplies.

Always wipe-up liquid spills immediately and caution others to be careful in the wet area. Following the pet bathing safety rules will keep the tub area clean. DO NOT use a vacuum for wet spills.

Clean the work area of pet hair and other waste after each household. Place refuse in a waste container lined with a trash bag. Before disposing the bag tightly seal it to prevent spilling.

All waste containers and vacuum cleaners are to be emptied at the end of every business day.
Always leave the area clean for the next person.
Be sure the clean-up checklist is completed daily.

The above procedure covers in detail miscellaneous items related to the cleaning policy that may not be covered on the posted checklists. Checklists are laminated and posted in the workplace available for all. Copies of all checklists are also posted to the handbook. Some employers require lists to be dated and signed daily for accountability. Laminated sheets can be checked and signed with dry-erase marker. Then a picture can be submitted via text or email to the supervisor leaving the list ready for the next user.

Training Employees

All staff, including owners and managers, should have an ongoing training program. It need not be formal but can certainly become a robust curriculum, if desired. You will have to decide what works best for your ideals and budget. Yes, education can be expensive, however, it pays dividends in the future and will keep your company on the cutting edge.

The business should pick up at least a percentage of training costs and continuing education. It is tax deductible and can also be part of your benefits package. Unfortunately, things that are obtained for "free" often hold less value for the consumer. In this case, the employee is the consumer. If they are signed up for a class and 100% of the cost has been paid by their employer, they may have less incentive to optimally perform or worse, they may not show up for the session. Therefore, if you offer to reimburse a portion, say 40-60% of the cost, the employee has a stake in the game. Another option would be to allow the employee to pay for their own training and the business can offer a bonus for course completion. At the very least, allow them to take the time off to pursue these endeavors.

In the very beginning, Mary made mention that she was grateful to the nationally-branded company for giving her a chance, but also ticking her off enough to quit and start her own business. We wanted to go to Groom Expo in 2001. And all Mary asked of them was to not make her take vacation time. She paid for all for classes and travel plus an add-on pet first aid class. Well, they made her take her vacation time. After the pet first aid class, she was talking to the instructor who informed her that he had just taught all the upper corporate management the very course that she paid extra for. Mary went to the show floor and put a deposit down on a mobile grooming van.

Many employers question, "why should I pay for their education when they can take it with them" and "I am just paying to improve my competition." You will not be a successful manager, boss, or owner with that kind of outlook. The owner should want to empower every member of the company to be their best self. Remember, when employees are successful, the company is successful! Knowledge IS power, it is the stuff a stellar team is made up of. Don't you want your business to be the best? Education is the key.

Not all training is expensive. You can create your own programs based on how you want job functions performed. You have already created the foundation while documenting your systems and generating your handbook. Be sure to keep these resources up to date. Other suggestions for economical education/training are in the "Continuing Your Education" section of this book.

Evaluations

Evaluations are a great way to uncover what areas need to be improved and where an individual has achieved mastery. It is important to administer evaluations on a regular basis. Every 3 months may be needed for a new hire. A veteran staff member should be evaluated at least annually. Of course, this includes the owner and business too such as with client surveys and SWOT analyses.

Evaluations are concrete tools that can be the basis for a raise or promotion. They should represent the trend over a given period, not one single day. We all have outstanding and lackluster days; neither should define overall performance. The evaluation should be presented to the employee in a private meeting. They should sign the document to show they have read and understand its contents. There should also be a section for them to note their thoughts, reactions, and future goals. The report is to be kept in the employee's personnel file for future reference.

The goals set forth in any evaluation should be "SMART" goals. The acronym "SMART" stands for Specific, Measurable, Achievable, Realistic and Time-bound. Adhering to these guidelines will help you to set successful goals.

Avoiding Isolation

Another consideration for employees or even yourself is isolation. It can be difficult to cope with. It is the very reason some groomers do not go mobile. Mobile employees can feel disconnected from the company and their co-workers because they are not a part of the regular day-to-day activities of the office and often do not have the opportunity to interact with one another as in a shop. To help address this issue, consider instituting regular staff meetings and dinners, allowing workers to share stories from their work on the road. Create team-building activities that include the entire work-force. Consider giving employees an opportunity to discuss challenges and solutions. It is important that all feel valid and valuable. These strategies should be designed to strengthen camaraderie, boost morale, and reinforce your business's culture.

Worker Classification

Once you have decided to hire staff it is vital to classify workers appropriately. Incorrect classification is a crime which can carry hefty fines and unnecessary aggravation. These fines can be so great, they can force a business to close its doors permanently.

The majority of stylist job arrangements in the grooming industry are employer-employee. Many employers incorrectly classify the groomer as an independent contractor because of perceived tax and insurance liability relief. In short, it appears to be cheaper and easier to label the person an independent contractor or "IC." Proper classification is needed to ensure everyone is adequately covered when the unexpected happens, and to be certain Uncle Sam gets paid.

At first, it may seem like a gray area but, upon further exploration, there are clear differences between the designations. For the sake of simplicity, the defining difference between an employee and an independent contractor comes down to who is in control. In the case of an employee, **the employer has the legal right to control the details of how the services are performed**. This applies even if one is given freedom of action. An independent contractor has the right to control all aspects of work including what and how it will be done. Other characteristics of an employer/employee arrangement are: permanency of the relationship, employee has little relative investment in facilities and typically, a non-compete relationship. Other characteristics of an independent contractor are: they are self-employed, discrimination laws and benefits do not apply, they are responsible for paying their own taxes and carrying their own insurances.

There are specific criteria set forth by the IRS to determine if someone is an employee, or an independent contractor: irs.gov/businesses/small-businesses-self-employed/independent-contractor-self-employed-or-employee

Still, some insist on knowingly improperly classifying employees as ICs. They believe the benefits outweigh the risks. These individuals are leaving themselves vulnerable to a random government audit and to the whims of their staff. All it takes is one complaint from a disgruntled employee to the department of labor to set the wheels of destruction in motion.

"I don't have IC's or pay ANYTHING under the table. Not only is it illegal it is not in anyone's best interest."
    ~ Beth

Employee Compensation

This is always a hot button issue. There are many ways to approach compensating your staff. It should not be a random number that most people use as the standard way of doing business. You need to understand why you are willing to pay what you pay. Once you have an intimate understanding you can easily explain your methods to others.

As with pricing, it must be based on real numbers and what you feel a fair wage is for the work being done. Would you do the job with the quality you expect for the amount you are offering? If the answer is no, you NEED to reevaluate your compensation structure. There are many different levels of competence, and your system needs to account for those differences. It is not fair to pay all staff the same across the board and it is not fair to your business to pay someone the same that delivers less.

The most common ways to pay an employee are hourly, salary, commission, and combinations thereof. Each system has strengths and weaknesses. Combinations cultivate synergy and emphasize benefits while minimizing deficits. That is why combinations are preferable.

Let's explore the pro's and con's. Hourly rates establish a baseline amount for compensation. An hourly rate is often used for purposes such as new hires, continuing education, paid time off, reimbursement for lost wages etc. Minimum hourly wages are legally protected. Be sure to know the current rate and have a viable time-keeping system. There are numerous apps available for this purpose Unfortunately, employees paid solely by this method tend to be uninspired and may drag their heels to complete a task.

Some feel salary is the easiest way to compensate. Some feel it is a desirable way to be paid. Salaries are consistent and do not vary, making budgeting much easier. Although it is very straight forward, it is difficult to reward outstanding staff. People may feel taken advantage of during busy times and unfortunately, some are motivated to underperform with this model. Also, it does not allow for incidentals such as staff meetings etc.

Commission is the industry standard. A commission structure is flexible, allows for job splitting, and can be a sliding scale to reflect a worker's performance level. The percentage can be adjusted to reward OR penalize the employee. This model incentivizes staff member to work their hardest. Conversely, it can encourage them to rush or compromise quality. Furthermore, commission-only is not a legal option in every state.

Combinations of systems ensure all are fairly and legally paid. The essential point, no matter where you're located, is that all employees must receive at least the minimum wage for their time, and time-and-a-half for more than 40 hours in any given week **calculated weekly**. Minimum wage varies by state and sometimes by county. Stay current on minimum wage amounts.

"The way I compensate my groomers is based on a commission

amount, then broken down to a combination of hourly and performance bonus. For example: I have a sliding scale based on sales per day from 35% to 45%. Let's say the day's sales are $500 from an 8-hour work day. The employee's gross pay will be $225 which is 45% of daily sales. However, for labor compliance, the employee's paycheck reads hourly earnings of $196 ($12 my current minimum wage) and bonus earnings of $129 for a gross total of $225." ~ Beth

Do yourself a favor and hire a payroll company to do payroll, unless you REALLY WANT to do your own payroll. Hiring a payroll firm is money well spent doing an important task you may not feel comfortable processing. They will also make sure you are legally compliant and ensure all taxes are handled. Most large payroll processing firms offer benefits such as medical and retirement planning for their clients.

Benefits are an extension of compensation. Though they are not mandatory, they show good will and that you appreciate your team members. Common benefits may include but are not limited to; continuing education, retirement saving/planning, paid time off and medical. Many small grooming businesses do not offer simple benefits such as paid time off. This is unfortunate. Burnout is ever present in our industry. Regular paid time off greatly increases morale and productivity. Even a modest benefits package will make your firm more attractive to prospective employees and increase employee retention.

Discipline and Termination

As issues arise, and they will, take the opportunity to use them as learning exercises. Don't avoid discipline-based conversations. They may be uncomfortable; however, they are tremendous opportunities to grow and become a better team. Many employees fail because of poor leadership. If you hope to be a good boss, it is your job to offer guidance, support and feedback.

We tend to learn more from our failures than our successes. This is a game vs. war, albeit a high-stakes game. Strategy has a more positive connotation that can boost enthusiasm and teamwork. War is a negative concept that will breed distrust and contempt and will eat away at the foundation of your business. You want your staff to respect you, not fear you. Staff will perform better for a supervisor they trust and want to please.

Before you develop your company's discipline and termination guidelines, be sure to consult federal and state departments of labor. Each have strict guidelines for hiring and firing processes. It is imperative to remain compliant with their protocols to avoid fines and litigation.

When correcting a team member, cite in the handbook where they went wrong. Remind them they agreed to uphold the policies and procedures outlined in the handbook. This helps to reinforce that the handbook is an excellent resource for problem solving. Typically, a verbal reminder will suffice. When that is not enough, a second warning should be presented to the team member in writing. If a third warning is required for moderate misconduct, they are again presented with a "write-up" and notified that further wrongdoing may result in compensation modification or termination. Gross misconduct such as violence in the workplace is grounds for immediate termination. As always, document the incident and include local law enforcement, if necessary. All levels of discipline should be outlined in the employee handbook as well.

At some point it will be necessary to take disciplinary action to correct unwanted habits, actions, and attitudes. It may be as simple as letting them know they have disappointed you. This may be all this is required IF you have taken the time to earn your staff's respect and have learned how to appeal to their desire to please. Sometimes you may have to up the ante and use more impactful tools such as additional duty assignments, temporary reduction in earnings/hours, or unpaid suspension.

Termination is the last resort. Typically, it is far more expensive to hire a new employee than it is to keep an existing staff member. You should carefully weigh your options and the impact on the wellbeing of your business, personnel, as well as yourself before making a final decision. This is NOT the time nor place for rash, emotionally-charged thinking. If you need time to sort your thoughts and feelings, suspend the employee from active duty for a period of no more than one week. This affords ample time to come up with a well-thought-out conclusion. If they won't give you the time, the decision is made for you; they should be let go. NEVER allow yourself to be bullied into any determination. If so, then who is really in charge?

When it is clear termination is necessary, immediately begin the separation process. Change all passwords, combinations, locks and cancel all cards the person can access. Inform the former staff member the last check will be sent when all company equipment has been accounted for. You may want to make a public announcement, "regrettably", the individual is no longer with your company. You must try to protect all aspects of the business from a resentful former employee.

A notice formally terminating employment should be written and distributed to the former employee. It should clearly detail the reason for ending their employment. Misconduct, absence without leave or abandonment of duties are a few examples. The letter should also contain the date employment was terminated. It should contain only the facts and supporting details.

Always maintain complete professionalism throughout this process. It is a business decision made only with your company's welfare considered. All documents may be submitted into legal proceedings. They should not contain personal notes, unpleasantries, or opinion.

Most folks prefer to use quick methods of communication. Thankfully, gone are the days of drawn-out telephone conversations. I try to document most interactions, whether with clients or employees. Creating a dialogue record via email or text message is now very easy. There are many apps that can be used to back up and or restore text messages to your email account.

These records are invaluable when settling perceived miscommunications. All disciplinary interactions must be noted and stored in the employee's file. It is easy for a situation to become fuzzy or forgotten if not properly re-counted. The better your records, the more informed your decisions would be. Should the situation require legal proceedings such as unemployment claims or a lawsuit, comprehensive documentations would increase your chances of a favorable outcome.

"The hardest thing I have done since opening my business is to let someone know they're fired." ~ Beth

7

Come Full Circle

GOAL:
Make decisions how to fulfill
your endgame.

"Good business leaders create a vision, articulate the vision, passionately own the vision, and relentlessly drive it to completion."

~ Jack Welch

What's Your Endgame?

Nothing lasts forever. Not our bodies nor the enterprise you have or hope to build. It is wise to start this venture with an eye on the finish line. That way you can set appropriate goals and can determine what will be needed to meet your goals. The finish line will look different for each individual and, of course. your vision will likely morph with time.

Looking ahead can be difficult because who knows what life will throw in our midst? With a clear vision and plan, you will be able to manage unexpected detours more easily while keeping your focus. Some resist looking ahead because the thought of the future can be overwhelming, but if you fail to plan you plan to fail.

It is very important to save for retirement as early as possible. The earlier in life one begins to save for retirement, the more resources they should have available for their golden years. The amount set aside per check, week, month, or year need not be a vast amount. However, if you wait until later in life, you will need to save larger amounts because there will be less time to accrue funds. It is not wise to count on inheritance to sustain your retirement. Those resources are not yours to make plans with nor are there guarantees you will receive them when needed or even at all.

Beth's Endgame:

"I prefer to err on the side of caution. Therefore, I assumed Social Security would not be available when I come of age. Also, I stopped contributing to Social Security VERY early. Pretty Paws was born in my early 20's, I was officially self-employed and no longer required to pay into the system. So, if I do receive Social Security it surely will not be enough to live on. It was obvious there would need to be other sources of income.

My financial advisor impressed upon me it was/is very important to have a mixed plan with varied sources. So, I was sure I did not put all my eggs in one basket. I started contributing to a 401k at the age of 18. The earlier in life one begins to save for retirement, the better. In addition, my business offers a company sponsored IRA to all eligible employees, including the owner, and matches a designated percentage for each participant. Along with those accounts, investing in real estate, being the beneficiary of several insurance policies with my husband as well as a recipient of his pension, I feel I have a healthy retirement plan. I also do not intend to cease working altogether so any funds derived from teaching and consulting will be icing on the cake."

Retirement benefits are very attractive to prospective employees and ensures current staff members their company cares about their well-being and future. Most savings plans have tax benefits, so be sure to search out all possible rewards.

Take the time to envision what you want the business to look like when you retire, assuming you want to retire. What does retirement mean to you? Perhaps it means being free from technical grooming, but you still want to run the administration of the business. Some folks want to have nothing to do with work in their retirement. Perhaps, you would like to teach, write, or do consulting work. You have acquired sought after skills during your career as a pet care professional, if desired, you can have those skills pay dividends in retirement by using them however it suits you and your wallet. No specific scenario is right or wrong, you just need to decide what you want. Then form a measurable plan of how to achieve your goals.

Hiring a reputable financial planner can be extremely helpful in setting your retirement dreams in motion. These professionals can give you general guides or a detailed plan tailored to your needs. Their services can be very basic or extremely detailed. Realize this is planning for your future financial well-being and don't skimp!

More on Beth's Endgame:
"From the beginning I knew I wanted a fleet of grooming units and employees. I wanted to semi-retire early in life by grooming 1-2 days per week, eventually leading to full retirement. To me, full retirement means being

completely free of Pretty Paws and technical grooming. Whether that means selling the business in whole or parts has yet to be determined. As is the exact timing of when full retirement will occur.

It is difficult to envision life without this industry. I love this business and have poured my heart and soul into pet care. That is why I teach and privately consult. These tasks are not labor intensive and can continue to be a viable source of entertainment, enrichment, and income."

If you don't intend to pass on the business as a gift, you will have to prepare to sell. Again, that is why it is important to know how you intend to close shop. Just another example of why it is extremely important to keep accurate detailed financial records. Many make the mistake of employing "creative" bookkeeping practices. Fudging the company's numbers will not serve you well in this and many other cases. You can not sell the business for what it is truly worth if your figures are not authentic.

While on the topic of selling the business and its assets the client list is one of the biggest assets a company has, without clients there is no business. It may or may not be legal in your locale to sell client information by itself. However, it may be legal to bundle the list into the sale of the business increasing its value. Be sure to check local regulations before making this decision. Be sure to base your sale value on empirical evidence not what you "think" its worth.

Mary's Endgame:

"I choose to offer my considerable expertise through an online membership program, as well as online and onsite individual workshops for pet professionals."

However, you decide to plan for the future, plan as early as possible.

Selling Your Mobile Unit

Selling your unit may be an emotionally-charged decision. Sometimes attachments are formed to the equipment. But as with any relationship, there is a beginning and end. Some folks may decide to hold on to their unit till it "dies" then sell the parts to salvage. Some may decide to donate it to charity for the tax write-off. Still, other units are sold well before their "best by" date and can be used as a piggy bank.

Many folks are not good with saving money, choosing to spend all that is available and hoping for the best in the end. "Failing to plan is planning to fail." There is an entire chapter dedicated to retirement planning in this book. Selling a gently used unit can dovetail with many saving strategies. Selling a used unit can provide a sizeable amount of money for financial investments such as contributions for 401K's or IRA's, buying real estate, investing in the stock market, or purchasing bonds. Whatever you decide to do with the proceeds, you must approach this task carefully and with due diligence.

When is the best time to sell? There is no straightforward answer to that question. It all depends what your situation calls for. Some have life-changing situations that dramatically alter circumstances, forcing the business to close or suspend operations. Sometimes a business outgrows the current unit. Some may sell after warranty expiration and some may hold-out till repairs become too much to deal with.

Whatever your circumstances, look at this venture as just another business decision. Do not allow yourself to get emotionally invested in the process. Research similar vehicles and units to get a general idea of how to price the unit. Do not go solely on those numbers. Consider what options your unit has as well as the condition, miles (when applicable), and whether you have all service documents. If your unit was converted by a company, call them and ask their opinion of the current resale value.

It is always important to take good care of your unit. This includes regular cleaning inside and out as well as adhering to all recommended maintenance intervals. You should keep a file on each unit that contains ALL related paperwork. Keeping every shred, both digital and hard-copies, greatly increases the resale value of your unit.

Once you have a general idea of how much to ask, decide how much you are willing to take. What is your bottom line? It is important to know that number because it's easy to get caught up in negotiations, resulting in accepting less than you want or need just to make the sale. Even when the price is listed as "firm", most folks expect to negotiate. So, leave some wiggle room when possible. If you are looking to get rid of the unit yesterday, price it at the lowest acceptable number and be sure to convey the price is not negotiable.

Try to be patient. Just as when clients call to price-shop, you will likely entertain conversations with individuals who are not serious. These conversations can easily waste your time. Keep all conversations professional and on-topic. It is reasonable and important to inquire from the beginning how the prospective buyer expects to pay for the unit. This will help determine if the inquiry is serious. If you do not get genuine inquires within 4-6 weeks of posting, you may have to revisit, and perhaps, adjust your asking price.

Where and How to List Grooming Units For Sale

First you must construct an informative ad. Include all aspects of your unit in the ad. This is the first contact you will have with potential buyers. WOW them with all the bells and whistles your unit has. Include the year, make, model, conversion company (if applicable), miles, how it is powered, recent repairs such as new tires or alternator, service records, etc. Also, be sure to disclose any work that needs to be done.

List the Ad Where the Groomers Are!

You may not get much interest generated from www.craigslist.com. Facebook groomer groups, www.petgroomer.com and www.usedgroomingvans.com are all excellent resources for selling used grooming units. Include as many high-quality photos as possible to show off the unit from all angles. Limit background distractions and ensure the images honestly show the condition of the unit. A prospective buyer will not have faith in doing business with you if you wait till they see the unit to disclose body or mechanical issues. If they have driven hours or days to view the unit, they will be rightfully upset if you have withheld pertinent information.

Once you have negotiated the selling price with the buyer, finalizing the sale is the last step. Before listing the van, you should know the location of the Title to the vehicle. Without this document the sale can not be completed. You may need to contact your state's Department Of Motor Vehicle to get a copy if you cannot find the original. The final meeting will entail turning over all documents to the buyer of the unit after the seller has received the full balance of the sale. It is imperative that all payment is secured before turning over owner-related documents.

If the buyer is financing or paying via bank wire, it is best for this transaction to take place at the bank. If a notary is required, there is typically one available at the bank branch. Do not turn over sensitive banking information to a buyer. Let the bankers handle that transaction for you. Do not accept personal checks or bank checks as payment on checks can be stopped at any time.

As always, cash is king. If you are to be paid in cash for the unit, exercise extreme personal safety. Have another trusted person present and make the exchange in a very public setting to reduce the possibility of assault.

Lastly, be sure to prepare two copies of a bill of sale for the unit. The bill of sale should plainly state that the unit is being sold "as is" and no guarantees are implied.

The bill should be signed by both parties and one copy remain with each party for tax purposes. Selling your unit may seem a daunting task but, if you take the time to prepare, it can be a very exciting experience.

Parting Thoughts

Mary's Parting Thoughts

Congratulations on your decision to go mobile! I've always thought we should have a sash such as the Girl Scouts have with badges sewn on. Only our badges would be for all the dumb things we do as mobile groomers. Before you beat yourself up, let me list the badges I would have on mine:

- Arriving at the wrong house.

- Arriving at the right house, but with no towels or empty water tanks.

- Towed out of someone's driveway when I misjudged the width and ended up in the soft mud alongside.

- Drove off with the back doors open.

- Drove off with the water hose still attached.

- Took out a mailbox, two basketball hoops, and low hanging wires across a driveway.

- Got a new client when I slid on some black ice into their vehicle.

- Forced a jogger up onto a snow bank when I slid on black ice.

I guarantee you I am not the only mobile groomer with this type of list.

I am available for consultations. Contact me for information, or to say hi at:

Mary@PawsitivelyPretty.com

Beth's Parting Thoughts

Now that you have taken the time to explore the vast world of mobile grooming, I hope you have concluded that you can make your business whatever you wish. There is no "right" or "wrong" way to do things. There is just your way and their way. Embrace those differences and follow your own unique path. There is no telling where it will lead!

For those of you already in business, kudos to you! Owning a mobile grooming business is not for the faint of heart. Congratulate yourself for seeking out more information in hopes of improving your operation. It is never too late to change or adjust your course. If you need to re-invent your company, I urge you to do so. Let your business work for you.

I'm sure you now know, I like to plan. I will say one last time, "if you fail to plan; you plan to fail." If you set measurable goals that compliment your vision and create a plan to achieve those goals, you will see results.

May the grooming "gods" smile upon you and bring you good fortune, few malfunctions and a good sense of humor.

For information on personal consulting or business coaching feel free to email:

Beth@prettypawsllc.com

Resources

Resources and Forms

To keep current with resources and forms for the mobile groomer, you will find them at:

www.PawsitiveEd.com/mobile-groomers-bible-resources

As of the printing of this book there are close to 30 forms. Such as but not limited to:

- Snout to Tail Assessment

- Matted Pet Release

- Receipt

- Pet Report Card

- Terms of Service

- Client Information

www.ingramcontent.com/pod-product-compliance
Lightning Source LLC
Chambersburg PA
CBHW072131020426
42334CB00018B/1748